Lady Katherine Knollys: The Unacknowledged Daughter of Henry VIII

Lady Katherine Knollys: The Unacknowledged Daughter of Henry VIII

Sarah-Beth Watkins

Winchester, UK
Washington, USA

First published by Chronos Books, 2015
Chronos Books is an imprint of John Hunt Publishing Ltd., Laurel House, Station Approach,
Alresford, Hants, SO24 9JH, UK
office1@jhpbooks.net
www.johnhuntpublishing.com

For distributor details and how to order please visit the 'Ordering' section on our website.

ISBN: 978 1 78279 585 8

A CIP catalogue record for this book is available from the British Library.

Design: Stuart Davies

Printed and bound by CPI Group (UK) Ltd, Croydon, CR0 4YY

We operate a distinctive and ethical publishing philosophy in all
areas of our business, from our global network of authors to
production and worldwide distribution.

CONTENTS

Chapter One - Mother Mary   1

Chapter Two - Aunty Anne   15

Chapter Three - Growing Up with Elizabeth and Mary   33

Chapter Four - Maid of Honour   43

Chapter Five - The Two Henrys   60

Chapter Six - Bloody Mary and the Exiles   76

Chapter Seven - Queen Elizabeth's Lady   93

Appendix - Of Her Blood   111

References   119

Bibliography   122

Books by Sarah-Beth Watkins

The Tudor Brandons
Catherine of Braganza
Ireland's Suffragettes
Margaret Tudor, Queen of Scots: The Life of
King Henry VIII's Sister

Books for Writers:
Telling Life's Tales
Life Coaching for Writers
The Lifestyle Writer
The Writer's Internet

Chapter One

Mother Mary

Mary Boleyn placed her hand on her stomach. It was time to shut herself away from the world and enter her darkened chambers. Richly embroidered tapestries lined the room, shutting out the light and keeping in the warmth from the banked-up fire. Mary was going to give birth to her first child; born of lust and passion, a child whose father was not the man she had married, a child whose father was secretly the King. A child she named Katherine.

Katherine would grow up never to be acknowledged as King Henry VIII's daughter. Henry had every reason not to acknowledge her. He had his daughters, one already born when Katherine came into the world, and he needed no more. His denial of his affair with Katherine's mother, Mary, would be something that would always position Katherine as a bastard. Yet Katherine joined the Tudor court as maid of honour to Queen Anne of Cleves and she went on to serve Catherine Howard as well as becoming one of Elizabeth I's closest confidantes - cousins for definite, more likely half-sisters. Katherine lived through the reigns of Henry VIII, Edward VI, Mary I and on into Elizabeth I's. Never far from court, she lived in a world where she would never be a princess but a lady she was born to be.

As a young girl, Katherine's mother, Mary journeyed to France in Mary Tudor's entourage, travelling in the same ship. At fourteen years old, it was a great adventure and her first time away from England. Her father had arranged for her to become a chamberer for the King's sister, a step down from a lady-in-waiting but her first position away from home. She must have looked up to the red-haired, delicately featured Mary who was being sent to marry the ageing King of France, Louis XII, with awe and respect. Here was a princess who was doing her duty for England by becoming Louis' third wife and Queen Consort of France.

They set sail on 2nd October 1514 crossing the Channel to Boulogne in a flotilla of 14 ships but a fierce storm made their journey last four days. Mary Tudor's ship ran aground and the women had to be carried to shore to meet the French ambassadors that were awaiting their arrival. All the women were windswept, soggy and seasick as they landed on the beach in such an unceremonious fashion. Not a good start to Mary's time in France.

From there, they travelled on to Abbeville where, on 9th October, the feast day of St Denis, Mary Tudor wed King Louis XII in the Hotel de la Gruthuse. The couple wore matching costumes of gold and ermine as they took part in the ceremony officiated over by the Bishop of Bayeux and Mary was bedecked in jewels that Henry had given her to show off England's wealth and riches.

The Venetian ambassador commented, 'The mass by the Cardinal de Bayeux being ended, he gave the consecrated wafer, one half to the King and the other to the Queen, who kissed and then swallowed it; and after making a graceful curtsey she departed, the King and Queen going each to their own apartments to dine. In the evening the Queen arrayed herself in the French fashion, and there was dancing; the whole Court banqueting, dancing, and making good cheer; and thus, at the eighth hour before midnight, the Queen was taken away from the entertainment by Madame to go and sleep with the King.

...She appears to me rather pale, though this I believe proceeds from the tossing of the sea and from her fright. She does not seem a whit more than 16 years old, and looks very well in the French costume. She is extremely courteous and well mannered, and has come in very sumptuous array...'[1]

When the fuss of the wedding had died down, King Louis

decided to rid Mary Tudor of most of her entourage, fearing that amongst them were spies who would report back to Henry VIII. When other servants were sent home, Mary Boleyn stayed on with the newly crowned Queen as she adjusted to her new life at the French court. King Louis had allowed Mary Tudor to retain only her six youngest maids but his control over Mary's household was short-lived. The King died just three months after Mary Tudor had arrived in France - some said from the exertions of his marriage bed - but not by being smothered to death by his new wife as a popular historical TV series would have us believe. Still the new Queen Consort Mary was not allowed home. Mary Boleyn stayed with her through the forty days of traditional mourning as all eyes were on Henry's sister waiting to see if she carried King Louis' child. When no pregnancy showed, Mary was allowed to return to England and Louis' son, François, was crowned King of France. But the ending of Mary Tudor's time in France was not without scandal. Knowing her brother, the King, would marry her off to the next politically advantageous suitor, she married his friend and confidant, Charles Brandon, whilst still in France thus enraging her brother, the King of England.

During this time, while Mary was attending Mary Tudor, her sister, Anne, who was yet to become the most infamous of the Boleyn family, was sent to the French court in service to François' wife, Claude, and is noted in records of the time but we lose sight of Mary for while her sister stayed at court, Mary's whereabouts are unknown. She may have travelled back to England and joined her mother in service to Queen Catherine of Aragon or she may have been sent to consider her actions if the rumours about her conduct were true.

This is the time in Mary's life where historians have surmised that she became the mistress of the new King François, giving her historical notoriety for being the sexual plaything of Kings. It is true she spent time at the court of King Louis but the suggestion she was a great and infamous whore came not from

François but from Rodolfo Pio, the Bishop of Faenza, who wrote "per una grandissima ribald et infame sopre tutte" - 'for a very great whore, and infamous above all'[2]. Pio was the Papal Nuncio in Paris and as such would have been extremely biased against the Boleyns when he wrote this some twenty years after Mary's time in France. Mary was at the court of the King Louis XII from around 1514 - 1515 and she may well have been his son's mistress for a time but there is no other evidence for it or that she was passed on to his companions as a sexual plaything as some writers have indicated.

Wherever she was, Mary next appears at the English court of King Henry and she might have caught his eye by being in service to the Queen as many of Henry's other women did. Henry was not the notorious womaniser he has been made out to be at this time but he had just come out of a relationship with Elizabeth Blount, or Bessie, as she was known, the daughter of Sir John Blount and Catherine Pershall of Kinlet near Bridgnorth in Shropshire, who was one of Queen Catherine's maids-of-honour.

In 1519 Bessie was sent to 'Jericho' to give birth to the King's illegitimate son. This was an affair that had lasted some time and resulted in the birth of a child that Henry did acknowledge, unlike Katherine. Jericho was a private, moated house leased by the King from St Lawrence's Priory at Blackmore, Essex. It was a house of poor reputation, a meeting place for the King and his lovers where the pages and grooms were warned 'not to hearken or enquire where the King is or goeth, be it early or late'. Bessie gave birth to Henry Fitzroy (Fitzroy meaning son of the king) on 15th June. Henry Fitzroy later became the Duke of Richmond and Somerset and Earl of Nottingham, reaping the rewards of an illegitimate but acknowledged son. Henry may have accepted his first male offspring but he wanted nothing more to do with Bessie and she was married off to Gilbert Tailboys in the same year of Henry's birth. The King had started to look for someone else to warm his bed.

Mary Boleyn was his choice. Her red hair, pert lips and wide eyes suggested innocence and succour at a time when Henry was troubled by his marriage to the Queen and his lack of any legitimate male heirs. Mary represented youth when Catherine was visibly ageing and the strain of several miscarriages and still-births were taking their toll on her body. Catherine was heading for the menopause and Henry was beginning to realise that his wife would never give him what he held most dear - a son to follow him to the throne.

Katherine's mother, Mary, became Henry VIII's lover at a time when Henry was in his prime. The life and soul of the Tudor court and England, Henry was a larger than life King, young and virile, enjoying all the pleasures of his sovereignty. He had not yet received the wound that would blight his later years and still enjoyed the pleasures of court; hunting, jousting, playing tennis and admiring women with his notions of courtly love.

In 1522, with all the panache and intrigue of a courtly love affair, Henry made his affections clear towards Mary at a joust held to welcome visiting ambassadors sent by the Emperor Charles V to negotiate a marriage between himself and the Princess Mary, Henry's daughter by Catherine of Aragon. Henry rode a horse whose caparisons were embroidered with the motto *Elle mon coeur a navera* - she has wounded my heart. Henry was in pursuit of Mary but his motto hints that the love was unrequited. Henry was in pursuit but perhaps Mary wasn't such a pushover as some historians have led us to believe. Certainly if the rumours of Mary and François did have any truth in them and her return to England had been in disgrace, she would hardly have been willing to risk that disgrace again. She was now a married woman and would have her husband's feelings to consider.

In that Easter's Shrove Tuesday celebrations, Mary played the role of Kindness in the pageant *The Assault on the Castle of Virtue* along with seven other women at court including her sister,

Anne, who took the role of Perseverance. The eight ladies of Kindness, Perseverance, Beauty, Honour, Constancy, Bounty, Mercy and Pity were mirrored by women (who were played by boys) of dubious qualities such as Danger, Jealousy, Unkindness, Scorn, Disdain, Malebouche (bad-mouthing), Strangeness and an eighth that is unrecorded. Eight lords had to rescue the women of good virtue from those that were dubious and amongst them was King Henry. The theme of the pageant was unrequited love and leading the lords who rescued the women was Ardent Desire. Although Henry did not take the main role, this was given to William Cornish, the court musician, its meaning was clear. Henry was in love and was pursuing a new mistress while still being married to Catherine of Aragon.

And Mary was married too so perhaps this affair would have less risk than his liaison with Bessie Blount. If any child were to be born, they would take Mary's husband's name and spare the King from having to acknowledge any more illegitimate offspring.

Mary had become the wife of William Carey on 4th February 1520. William Carey was the second son of Sir Thomas Carey of Chilton Foliat in Wiltshire, and his wife, Margaret Spencer, daughter of Sir Robert Spencer and Eleanor Beaufort. His aunt on the maternal side was Katherine Spencer, Countess of Northumberland, and through her, he was first cousin to Henry Percy, the 6th Earl of Northumberland, a former suitor of his sister-in-law Anne Boleyn. Katherine took William Carey's surname and William might never even have known of his wife's affair with the King but given his closeness to Henry he must surely have had his suspicions. It has been suggested that Henry VIII picked William as a compliant courtier to marry his mistress. He attended their wedding and gave the couple a gift of 6s 8d but William although compliant was not just an ordinary courtier. He had joined the King's household in 1519 and became close to the King through his role as a Gentleman of the Privy Chamber and Esquire of the Body to the King. As Mary's husband was a courtier in his own right, William was awarded grants from 1522 -1526 and this payment could have been for Mary's services. Whether through Mary's liaison with the King or because of his own merits, William did well out of the whole affair. In 1522, he was made keeper of the manor and estate of New Hall in Essex, a year later he was made chief steward and bailiff of the manor of Writtell and Writtell Park in Essex. The last grant William received came at around the time of the birth of Mary's second child, Henry Carey, in 1526 when William was made keeper of the manor, gardens and tower of Pleasance in Greenwich and granted the keepership of Ditton manor and park.

William may have just received grants because he was favoured by the King. Alternatively, he may have received them for being an obliging husband and to nurture his acquiescence while the King made love to his wife. Whatever the reason, both William and Mary were players in the King's game. They could not have refused him even had they have wanted to. Mary might well have endured the King's attentions but felt nothing for him or could she have felt genuine affection and been love-struck by such a king who at the time was in his magnificence? Either way she was left with two children who were rumoured to be the offspring of King Henry VIII.

Henry kept his affair with Mary a secret but his closest companions and men of his chambers knew what was happening. They collected Mary and took her to his rooms or arranged for their love trysts elsewhere. They may have met at Hever, Mary's family home, but that seems unlikely and there is no recorded evidence of him visiting her there although in 1521, Henry took possession of Penshurst Place which lay close to Hever and would have made a possible rendezvous point. Penshurst was a crenellated manor house set in idyllic surroundings. Built in the 14th century, beautiful countryside and surrounding parklands made it an impressive residence just a day's ride from London and the Tudor court. Mary may also have met Henry at Jericho where Bessie Blount had had her son and where he was known to meet with other women or Mary could have just been escorted to the King's rooms when he called for her. If Mary was travelling with the court and her husband, she would have been available wherever the King resided.

Henry not only failed to acknowledge Katherine, he also never once admitted to having an affair with Mary, but it is in his omission that we see his guilt. In 1533, a Catholic MP, George Throckmorton, in conversation with the King accused him of meddling with both Mary and her mother, Lady Boleyn. Henry replied, 'Never with the mother'. It took Thomas Cromwell to add 'Nor never with the sister either, and therefore put that out of your mind'. But this came at a time when Anne Boleyn was made Queen of England and to admit to relations with her sister would have had serious implications for their marriage. Henry had divorced Catherine of Aragon based on her previous relationship with his brother, Arthur. To admit that he had had close relationships with Mary would make his marriage to Anne incestuous. As we shall see later, this is why Katherine was never acknowledged as Henry's child as to do so was to jeopardise his marriage to her aunt.

Mary was sleeping with the King but surely she was aware of the risks. Did she try to do anything to prevent her pregnancy? Contraception in Tudor times was illegal and methods for preventing pregnancy were not reliable. Women sometimes used pessaries made from wool and soaked in vinegar, herbs, beeswax or even stones and wooden blocks to prevent conception. Essences of mint, rue or savin (a type of juniper) were drunk as abortants but could be deadly in high doses. Failing that, amulets were worn to ward off fertility and were as bizarre as the testicles of a weasel or the liver of a cat. If Mary had tried any of these, they had failed and with her belly extended before her, she entered the birthing chamber.

Mary took to her chamber four to six weeks before Katherine's birth and surrounded herself with good luck charms and she may even have used an eagle stone[3]. This was a time when superstition was rife and anything that could be done to ward off evil spirits and ensure a safe birth was done. An eagle stone - a hollow stone which has sand, a pebble or other noisy substance within it - was believed to help relieve labour pains during childbirth. As soon as her labour started, Mary's closest companions and the midwife were called. Men were not permitted in the birth chamber and there were no doctors as such to help with the birth.

The birthing chamber was the realm of the midwife, usually a respectable married woman, and not the dubious witch-like woman that is often depicted. The role of the midwife was to see her charge through labour and to supply the various ointments, poultices and herbal preparations needed to aid the child's birth, including pig fat to be used as a lubricant. This was a time of high mortality rates both for the mother and child and midwives were often called upon to baptise the newborn babe if it was thought they would not survive.

We don't know how long Mary was in labour for or how healthy Katherine was when she was born but both mother and baby survived against the odds of the time. Mary may have drunk the restorative drink, 'mother's caudle' - a spiced wine meant to give her renewed strength after the birth whilst Katherine was cleansed and swaddled as soon as she was born. Swaddling consisted of wrapping the baby in strips of linen or similar cloth to keep their bones straight and help them to grow up without physical deformity. The baby was kept immobilised by the cloth bands and also sometimes a swaddling board (or cradle board) for the first eight to nine months of their life, only being unbound to be cleaned and bathed.

Mary would have stayed in her bed in the darkened room for about three days after Katherine's birth until her 'upsitting' when she would begin to move about her chamber and receive more visitors. The norm was to stay in your chamber for a week or more before being allowed back into the household although not outside the house until the 'churching' ceremony had taken place. The churching ceremony was a way of purifying a woman where a short service would be held and the new mother would make an offering to the church which was wrapped in her newborn's christening gown. Unlike today, mothers did not attend their child's christening. They usually took place as quickly as possible and so were at a time when the mother was still confined to her birthing chamber.

Katherine was Mary Boleyn's first and only living daughter, born in 1524 at the height of her affair with King Henry VIII. There has been some conjecture over her date of birth - in Ive's study of Anne Boleyn, he suggests that her brother, Henry, was in fact the first born child of Mary Boleyn - but there is mounting evidence that Katherine was born in 1524 and Henry two years later. As births weren't recorded in the Tudor age, no certificates or Parish records exist but other evidence can be used to gauge when she was born.

The first piece of evidence is that she became a maid of honour to Anne of Cleves in 1539. This position was usually taken up by young girls at the age of sixteen or thereabouts and coincides with Katherine being in her early teenage years. The recent discovery of her husband's Latin dictionary, the first volume of a *Dictionarium Seu Thesaurus Latinae Linguae,* has provided the birth dates of Katherine and Sir Francis Knollys' 14 children and corroborated their date of marriage. Their last son, Dudley, was born in 1562 and this date coincides with a portrait believed to be of a heavily pregnant Katherine by Steven van der Meulen, whose inscription gives the sitter's age as 38. This confirms that if Katherine was 38 in 1562, she would have been born in 1524.

This portrait of Katherine is the only one that has been attributed to her. Art historians, Croft and Hearn suggest that there is 'a plausible resemblance between the sitter and the effigy of Lady Knollys' (Katherine's married name) in Rotherfield Greys church. It was sold at Sothebys by Katherine's descendents in the 1970s and as such its provenance proves it came from the Knollys family. As well as the portrait being attributed to Katherine, it also shows her resemblance to Henry VIII - the red hair, the same nose and a very similar set of the lips. Although we cannot go on looks alone, Katherine does show a remarkable likeness to Henry in this portrait and no resemblance to William Carey at all.

When Mary took to her birthing chamber, where was she? Some sources indicate that Mary gave birth in Hampton Court Palace while she was attending on Queen Catherine of Aragon as a lady-in-waiting, although as Wolsey didn't grant King Henry the palace until at least 1525, this would have been difficult, while others believe she was confined in her husband William's childhood home at Chilton Foliat. It seems unlikely that if Mary was indeed pregnant with the King's child that she would have gone to her husband's ancestral home for her confinement but then his family may never have known about her affair with the King. Although it became general knowledge in later years, at the time it was conducted with great secrecy. She may have given birth in any one of the King's residences whilst there with her husband, secluded herself away at Jericho as Bessie Blount had done or returned home to Hever to present her parents with their first grandchild.

We will never know how much King Henry pushed Mary into the affair but he was definitely capable of taking a woman by force should he so desire. An incident recorded in the State Papers tells us of one William Webbe who was charged with treason because he had 'cried vengeance on the King'[4]. He only did so because the woman he had been travelling with caught the King's eye. Henry kissed her and made her ride off with him, to become one of his mistresses or so William thought. Mary may have had no choice but to succumb to the King's attentions.

Mary continued her affair with Henry VIII after Katherine's birth which has lent further credence to him being her father. Henry forbade his mistresses to sleep with their husbands while they were in a relationship with him. He would not have taken her back if she'd just given birth to her husband's child.

In 1526, Katherine's brother, Henry, was born and by this time, Mary's affair with the King was over and his attentions had turned towards her sister, Anne. In one of Henry VIII's letters to Anne Boleyn he says '...also that I will take you for my mistress, casting off all others that are in competition with you, out of my thoughts and affection...'[5]. Was this Henry's way of letting Anne know that her sister, Mary, now meant nothing to him?

Mary was no longer a royal mistress and was soon to be a widow. She had not profited from her time with the King and when her husband, William Carey died of the sweating sickness in 1528, he was just 32 years old. Mary Boleyn was now a single mother with two children of questionable parentage. Mary was in dire straits.

Katherine's aunt Anne, who was high in the King's favour by now, interceded on their behalf. In King Henry's letter to Anne concerning their situation, he says 'As touching your sister's matter, I have caused Walter Welche to write to my lord mine mind therein, whereby I trust that Eve shall not have the power to deceave Adam. For surely, whatsoever is said, it cannot so stand with his honour, but that he must needs take her his natural daughter now in his extream necessity.'[6]

Sir Thomas Boleyn, father of both Anne and Mary, was told to allow Mary to return to the family home to live with her disapproving mother and her ageing grandmother, Lady Margaret Butler. Katherine too, was to return with her mother to the family home at Hever Castle where she would reside for the next five years of her life. The King also granted Mary a yearly annuity of £100 and it has been suggested this was primarily to make sure that Katherine was well looked after.

Mary had had a difficult relationship with the formidable Sir Thomas. Some historians have berated Thomas for using his daughters as bargaining chips to gain financial rewards and prestige, prostituting first Mary and then Anne in a callous bid to rise high in the King's favour but he was a typical Tudor man in that he saw his daughters as women who were under his control; they were his property to do with as he saw fit even if that included bringing his daughters to the attention of the King. Mary and Anne may well have caught the King's eye without any encouragement from their father.

In the girls' early days, he definitely took care to make sure they were well educated and sent to further their education by attending at foreign courts but in later years, he fell out with Mary and watched as Anne's momentous downfall took place. Sir Thomas took part in the trial that condemned Anne for her supposed actions without even once trying to save his daughter from her fate. We will never know how much his daughters' involvement with the King was out of his hands or whether he really did push them to catch Henry's eye. For both Mary and Anne, the consequences of their liaisons would be disastrous.

Returning to the family home of Hever Castle, near Edenbridge in Kent, must have been an upsetting journey for Mary and Katherine, now four years old. Hever was a 13th century castle of the Norman de Hever family. Sir Thomas' ancestor, Sir Geoffrey Boleyn made his money in trading in mercantile London and bought both Blickling and Hever estates for his family. When Thomas' father, Sir William, died in 1505, he was left the estates as his father's heir. He gave Blickling to his brother, James, and concentrated on making Hever Castle a family residence. He continued the renovation of Hever Castle to a manor house as started by his ancestors, specifically adding a 90ft long gallery above the great hall to be used as an area for exercise during bad weather when hunting or riding was not permissible.

The running of Hever Castle was conducted by Lady Elizabeth, Katherine's grandmother, who was rarely at court whether due to her own preference or Sir Thomas' orders. There would have been a steward to help collect rents or deal with tenants' disputes and many other servants to ensure the smooth running of the Boleyn home. Lady Elizabeth would have been responsible for overseeing the servants and making sure her home was well-kept and everybody's needs were catered for, including Mary and her daughter, Katherine. Lady Elizabeth may not have welcomed home two more mouths to feed, nor might she have been happy to see her disgraced daughter, and Katherine surely felt the tension between her grandmother and mother as she was growing up. It would be an uneasy start for a woman who was to become a Lady in her own right.

Katherine would never be afforded the luxury of being called princess but in Tudor times, being a princess wasn't a safe and secure position. Nor did it bring happiness to either of the Princesses Mary and Elizabeth, Henry's acknowledged daughters, especially throughout their childhood. The next few tumultuous years would see Katherine watching from the sidelines as the Tudor age unravelled and the fate of her once helpful aunt Anne was sealed.

Chapter Two

Aunty Anne

We will never know how Katherine's mother felt about her sister, Anne Boleyn, usurping her in the King's affections. Was it a relief to no longer be the bedfellow of the King of England or did Mary miss her life at court? Did Katherine watch in horror as her aunt became the most talked about woman in Christendom and subsequently lose her life in a mass of intrigue and political manoeuvring? It was an upbringing that would have shocked any child and could have meant their disgrace from court but Katherine was always welcome.

King Henry was pursuing Katherine's aunt, Anne Boleyn, from as early as 1526. In February of that year, as he had done with Mary, he attended a joust riding a horse whose caparisons were embroidered with a message from his heart. This time he was wearing the motto 'Declare I dare not' along with a depiction of a heart surrounded by flame. At this time, the King's courtship of Katherine's aunt was in its early stages. Henry had no intention at this time of making Anne his next wife but Anne had other ideas. She had seen how Katherine's mother, her sister, was treated and refused to accept her role just as a mistress. She kept Henry dangling, never giving in to his protestations of love but encouraging him nonetheless. When the going got tough, she retreated to Hever and provoked a flurry of ardent letters and gifts.

Henry could not bear to be parted from Anne. She was rapidly becoming constant in his thoughts. He wrote to her:

My Mistress and friend, my heart and I surrender ourselves into your hands, beseeching you to hold us commended to your favour, and that by absence your affection to us may not be lessened: for it would be a great pity to increase our pain, of which absence produces enough and more than I could ever have thought could be felt, reminding us of a point in astronomy which is this: the longer the days are, the more distant is the sun, and nevertheless the hotter; so it is with our love, for by absence we are kept a distance from one another, and yet it retains its fervour, at least on my side; I hope the like on yours, assuring you that on my part the pain of absence is already too great for me; and when I think of the increase of that which I am forced to suffer, it would be almost intolerable, but for the firm hope I have of your unchangeable affection for me: and to remind you of this sometimes, and seeing that I cannot be personally present with you, I now send you the nearest thing I can to that, namely, my picture set in bracelets, with the whole of the device, which you already know, wishing myself in their place, if it should please you. This is from the hand of your loyal servant and friend, H.R.[1]

This letter shows a vulnerable side to Henry. He wanted Anne to return the love he felt for her but none of her letters remain for us to see her replies. However, her replies must have given the King hope as she did manage to keep him interested over the course of seven years before their marriage in 1533. At a private ceremony at Whitehall Palace, attended by few family and friends, Anne got what she had held out for, the hand in marriage of the King.

King Henry's infatuation with Anne resulted in his divorce from Queen Catherine of Aragon. They had been married for over twenty years and what is clear is that Henry desperately needed a son and heir which Catherine could no longer give him. The politics involved in the King's 'great matter' are long and convoluted and many authors have written volumes on this time in Henry's life.

What interests us here is how this related to Katherine's life as it directly impacts on why she was never acknowledged by her father. King Henry's main conviction in seeking a divorce from his Queen was that their marriage was frowned on in the eyes of God and was the reason why they had no sons (at least, no living sons). He quoted the bible - 'If a man shall take his brother's wife, it is an unclean thing he hath uncovered his brother's nakedness; they shall be childless' (Leviticus 20:21) - as confirmation that his marriage to Catherine was unwholesome. Henry had already made up his mind to put aside his wife but he was looking for proof and who could deny the word of God?

What was also at stake was his relationship to Anne if it became public knowledge that he had slept with her sister, Mary. If a marriage between a man and his brother's wife was so abominable then a marriage between a man and his mistress's sister was also. Leviticus also says 'Neither shalt thou take a wife to her sister, to vex her, to uncover her nakedness, besides the other in her life time' (Leviticus 18:18). Henry had placed himself within the 'first degree of affinity' or relatedness. To this end, we see another confirmation that Henry truly did have an affair with Mary when in 1527 he asked for a legal dispensation to remarry and to marry a woman with whom he had that first degree of affinity.

Even with a legal dispensation granted, others were aware of what Henry had done. His cousin, Cardinal Pole, went so far as to publish *Pro ecclesiasticae unitatis defensione (A Defence of the Unity of the Church)* which strongly accused him of having an affair with Mary and then getting rid of his wife so that he could marry Anne.

At your age in life, and with all your experience of the world, you were enslaved by your passion for a girl. But she would not give you your will unless you rejected your wife, whose place she longed to take. The modest woman would not be your mistress; no, but she would be your wife. She had learned, I think, if from nothing else, at least from the example of her sister, how soon you got tired of your mistresses; and she resolved to surpass her sister in retaining you as her lover.

Now what sort of person is it whom you have put in place of your divorced wife? Is she not the sister of her whom first you violated and for a long time after kept as your concubine? She certainly is. How is it then, that you now tell us of the horror you have of illicit marriage? Are you ignorant of the law which certainly no less prohibits marriage with a sister of one with whom you have become one flesh, than one with whom your brother was one flesh? If one kind of marriage is detestable, so is the other. Were you ignorant of the law? Nay, you knew it better than others. How did I prove it? Because, at the very time that you were rejecting your brother's widow, you were doing your very utmost to get leave from the Pope to marry the sister of your former concubine.

This treaty infuriated King Henry who wasn't used to being questioned and publicly attacked in this way. It also brought up the whole issue of his affair with Mary - *'for a long time after kept as your concubine'* that he had tried to keep secret but was now being brought into the open not just as a brief affair but one that had lasted some duration. It is precisely why Katherine would never be acknowledged by her father. His desire for her aunt overrode everything in his life at that time. To admit Katherine was his daughter, would admit his affair with her mother and thus jeopardise his marriage to the woman he wanted above all else.

Anne too may not have wanted Katherine to be acknowledged for her own reasons. Although she had a close relationship with her mother and her brother, George, she seems to have had little contact with Mary. She may even have despised her for being with the man she wanted as her husband. To know that she had had a child by the King must have galled her. She detested his other daughter, the Princess Mary, Henry's daughter by Catherine, and saw her sole mission as giving the King the legitimate heir he so wanted, making sure that he cast aside any other children, legitimate or not.

In many of the reports sent home by Chapuys, the Spanish ambassador, who was famous for his vitriol towards Anne, he writes of her animosity towards Catherine of Aragon and the Princess Mary. On the 10th October 1533, he reported that Mary's expenses and attendants had been reduced and by January 1534, he was telling of how Anne was insisting that Mary be kept in close confinement. There were even rumours that Anne might poison the King's daughter from his previous marriage. The act of divorce made the Princess Mary now the Lady Mary, in effect bastardising her, and Anne tried everything in her power to belittle her even further. And the King allowed this to continue. He was in no way blameless for the treatment of his first-born daughter. In Bernard's book about Anne Boleyn, he suggests that it is 'another example of Henry's skill at directing policy while allowing others to shoulder public responsibility for it.' Anne mistreated the Princess Mary but the King allowed her to do so which raises questions about how much he actually cared for his legitimate daughters let alone one who had been born to his mistress.

Katherine's aunt Anne was crowned as Queen on 1st June 1533 in Westminster Abbey with all the pomp and splendour her new role required. She was visibly pregnant but her robe of purple velvet covered her well. Her coronation was attended by the Boleyn family. The people of London had turned out to see her procession to the abbey but not in the droves she had expected. They laughed at their entwined initials 'HA' and there was a feeling of solemnity to the whole affair. Catherine of Aragon had been a well-loved Queen and Anne was her usurper. Chapuys, the Spanish ambassador, wrote that the coronation was 'a cold, thin and very unpleasant thing, to the great regret, anger and reluctance not only of the common people but also of all the rest. And it seems that the indignation of everybody about this affair has increased by a half since.'[2]

Anne was not a popular Queen for several reasons including her religious beliefs. Did she influence the King with her more progressive religious ideas? Certainly she introduced Henry to the writings of William Tyndale. She was interested in the reformation of religion and had lengthy discussions with some of the leading reformers of the times. She is known to have had a copy of the Bible in English which she encouraged her ladies to read.

Katherine may have been influenced by her aunt and her beliefs at such a young age but their contact seems to have been sparse. However, Katherine would uphold the protestant faith in her adult life and although this would be encouraged from her husband's side, it can be assumed that the basis for her beliefs also came from the maternal side of her family.

On 7th September 1533, the Princess Elizabeth was born at Greenwich - the daughter of Anne Boleyn and King Henry VIII, she was to play an all encompassing role in Katherine's life. Katherine was now 8 or 9 years old and still living at Hever as far as we can tell. Could she have any idea of how their lives would intertwine?

The King had wanted a boy, a male heir so Elizabeth was something of a surprise. Letters had been written announcing the arrival of a new prince to which a hastily scribbled 's' was added. Chapuys, being his usual malicious self, wrote, 'The King's mistress was delivered of a girl, to the great disappointment and sorrow of the King, of the Lady herself, and others of her party, and to the great shame and confusion of physicians, astrologers, wizards and witches, all of whom affirmed it would be a boy'.[3]

Within months, Elizabeth was sent to Hatfield although there is mention of Hertford Castle as the first choice for her residence. A household headed by Anne Shelton and Alice Clere was established and the three month old Elizabeth left London with some ceremony to journey to her new home. Anne was loath to see her daughter go but it was typical of the times for children to be sent from court and for princesses to have their own households.

Katherine packed up her belongings and set off for her new role as one of the many girls that would attend the new Princess Elizabeth. At one point Elizabeth's household was so overflowing with young women that her father Henry refused to let any more young girls attend her preferring more 'ancient and sad persons' to instil less frivolity into her upbringing.[4]

In Alison Weir's book about Katherine's mother, Mary Boleyn, she says, 'it is possible that Katherine...spent the next six years, until she was summoned to court, in her little cousin's household'. She echoes Sally Varlow's belief that 'Katherine probably spent the next six years in the household of her young "cousin"'. Elizabeth and Katherine were such firm friends in later years that they must have started that relationship during Elizabeth's early years. 'She was always one of the Queen's favourites and theirs was a friendship that had probably begun in childhood,' states Josephine Wilkinson in her book about Mary. Katherine would go on to be a lady-in-waiting to Anne of Cleves and Catherine Howard and then to flee England for Germany when Elizabeth's elder sister, Mary, took the throne. For Elizabeth to have such feeling for Katherine and vice versa, the girls must have spent time together at an early age.

Katherine was growing up between the ages of ten and fifteen, for at least part of the time, in a household of royal children and it is here that she would have met her other half-sister, Mary, and seen how both she and Elizabeth, her half-sisters, were treated and how they treated each other. Their relationship started on a rocky path and the atmosphere in the house would have been tense and uncomfortable. The political situation created by their father set his two acknowledged daughters at odds. Mary was no longer the Princess of the realm, Elizabeth had usurped her position and it made those that supported Catherine of Aragon and the Spanish alliance angry.

On 16th December 1533, Chapuys wrote of the baby Elizabeth's move to Hatfield House:

'According to the determination come to by the King about the treatment of the Princess and the bastard, of which I wrote in my last, the said bastard was taken three days ago to a house 17 miles from here ; and although there was a shorter and better road, yet for greater solemnity, and to insinuate to the people that she is the true Princess, she was taken through this town with the company which I wrote in my last ; and next day the duke of Norfolk went to the Princess to tell her that her father desired her to go to the Court and service of the said bastard, whom he named Princess. The Princess answered that the title belonged to herself, and to no other ; making many very wise remonstrances, that what had been proposed to her was strange and dishonorable. To which the Duke could not reply. After much talk, he said he had not come there to dispute, but to accomplish the King's will ; and the Princess, seeing that it was needless excusing herself, demanded half-an-hour's respite to go to her chamber, where she remained about that time, — to make, as I know, a protestation which I had sent her, in order that, if compelled by force or fraud to renounce her rights or enter a nunnery, it might not be to her prejudice. On returning from her chamber she said to the Duke that since the King her father was so pleased, she would not disobey him...'.[5]

Chapuys would always defend the Princess Mary, Queen Catherine's daughter, and in his eyes the Princess Elizabeth was the child of the usurper and therefore a bastard. Queen Catherine had been asked to accept the title of Princess Dowager of Wales when Anne was made queen but she refused to acknowledge it and always saw herself as Henry's true wife, and her daughter Mary as his true daughter borne in wedlock, but the Act of Succession in March 1534 reduced the Princess to Lady Mary and declared her a bastard. Chapuys was not only furious but concerned for Mary's safety. She was to join her sister at her new household at Hatfield and perhaps unbeknown to her meet her other half-sister, Katherine, as well.

Mary couldn't believe that her father would reduce her status after seventeen years of being treated as a Princess of the realm. When she was told of her new circumstances by Lord Hussey, Henry's new chamberlain, she remarked that she couldn't believe him 'without sufficient authorisation by commission or other writing from the King'. Mary refused to believe her father would treat her in such a way but Hussey returned to her with proof; a letter that ordered her to leave the country manor of Beaulieu in which she was referred to as 'the Lady Mary, the King's daughter'.[6]

Mary's own household was dissolved but she was allowed to take some of her servants to Hatfield with her. On her arrival at her new home, she was asked if she'd like to greet the new Princess to which she replied that 'she knew of no other princess in England but herself'. The move shocked and dismayed her and she wept uncontrollably at her new position. Mary was often unwell whether making herself sick or genuinely falling ill from the stress and turmoil of her changed circumstances. She was a fallen Princess and a teenage one at that. She refused to call Elizabeth Princess or acknowledge her as such. Her behaviour unsettled the otherwise calm of the nursery household although Elizabeth in her infancy was probably oblivious to her tantrums.

Hatfield House was a splendid decorative red brick house built around 1485 by John Morton, the Bishop of Ely, minister to Henry VII, as a Bishop's palace. It was an ideal house for a nursery with four wings that were arranged around a central courtyard, set in lush and pleasant gardens surrounded by a deer park in the Hertfordshire countryside. It was a place that Elizabeth would spend many years in as a child and during her sister, Mary's reign. In later days, she would receive news of Mary's death along with her ring here and the news that she was the new Queen of England.

Hatfield may have been Elizabeth's main residence but the girls travelled around to other country houses such as Hunsdon,

Hertford Castle and Ashridge. Ashridge was given to the young Elizabeth by her father, the King. Hunsdon, a moated house with deer park, was later to be given to Katherine's brother, Henry, by Elizabeth once she was Queen. It was deemed best for the royal children to be away from court and from an increased risk of disease and infection but they also visited the court at times in such places as Richmond, Greenwich and Eltham.

The new nursery household was governed by Sir John and Lady Shelton, an aunt of Anne Boleyn's, with Lady Bryan taking charge of Elizabeth's care. Lady Bryan had been a lady-in-waiting to Queen Catherine of Aragon and was made governess to the Princess Mary when she was born. She was held in high esteem by Henry VIII and was to be given the care of all the royal children in turn but for now, Elizabeth was her main charge.

Katherine would have witnessed the transference of affection from Mary to Elizabeth and Mary's subsequent differential treatment. No longer the Princess, Mary was treated with disdain and contempt. Even her father didn't wish to see her. In April 1534, the nursery moved to Eltham Palace, where Henry and Anne visited their daughter, Elizabeth. She was the one who received several visits from her parents during which Mary was shut out of sight, the forgotten daughter. While Anne was still Queen and in Henry's affections, Elizabeth was to be treated like the royalty she was. But this affection didn't last.

For Anne, her new role of Queen and mother was a whirlwind of activity but trouble was never far from the Boleyn family. The Lady Mary refused to acknowledge Anne as the Queen, seeing her mother as the only true Queen that she knew of. Whatever Anne tried, from having her ears boxed to insisting she took an inferior position in the Princess Elizabeth's household, Mary remained defiant. And this wasn't the only relationship that had turned sour. Anne and Mary Boleyn, Katherine's aunt and mother respectively, whilst never close, were to become even more estranged. Mary married Katherine's stepfather, William

Stafford, a soldier and spearman at the Calais garrison, without permission. It is said she appeared at court visibly pregnant although there are no records of this child and she may have miscarried or had a stillbirth. Anne was now the reigning Queen and she was both shocked and disappointed at Mary's actions. She sent the couple from the court in disgrace which prompted Mary to send a letter to Thomas Cromwell. From it we can see how she asked him to act on her behalf to bring Mary and her husband back into favour.

Master Secretary,

After my poor recommendations, which is smally to be regarded of me, that am a poor banished creature, this shall be to desire you to be good to my poor husband and to me. I am sure it is not unknown to you the high displeasure that he and I have, both of the king's highness and the queen's grace, by reason of our marriage without their knowledge, wherein we both do yield ourselves faulty, and do acknowledge that we did not well to be so hasty and so bold, without their knowledge. But one thing, good master secretary, consider, that he was young and love overcame reason; and for my part I saw so much honesty in him, that I loved him as well as he did me, and was in bondage, and glad I was to be at liberty: so that, for my part, I saw that all the world did set so little by me, and he so much, that I thought I could take no better way but to take him and forsake all other ways, and live a poor, honest life with him. And so I do put no doubts but we should, if we might once be so happy to recover the king's gracious favour and the queen's. For well I might have had a greater man of birth loved me so well, nor a more honest man; and besides that, he is both come of an ancient stock, and again as meet (if it was his grace's pleasure) to do the king service, as any young gentleman in his court.

Therefore, good master secretary, this shall be my suit to you, that, for the love that well I know you do bear to all my blood, though, for my part, I have not deserved it but smally, by reason of my vile conditions, as to put my husband to the king's grace that he may do his duty as all other gentlemen do. And good master secretary, sue for us to the king's highness, and beseech his highness, which ever was wont to take pity, to have pity on us; and, that it will please his grace of his goodness to speak to the queen's grace for us; for, so far as I can perceive, her grace is so highly displeased with us both that, without the king be so good lord to us as to withdraw his rigour and sue for us, we are never likely to recover her grace's favour: which is too heavy to bear. And seeing there is no remedy, for God's sake help us; for we have now been a quarter of a year married, I thank God, and too late now to call that again; wherefore it is the more almones to help. But if I were at my liberty and might choose, I ensure you, master secretary, for my little time, I have tried so much honesty to be in him, that I had rather beg my bread with him than be the greatest queen in Christendom. And I believe verily he is in the same case with me; for I believe verily he would not forsake me to be a king.

Therefore, good master secretary, seeing we are so well together and does intend to live so honest a life, though it be but poor, show part of your goodness to us as well as you do to all the world besides; for I promise you, you have the name to help all them that hath need, and amongst all your suitors I dare be bold to say that you have no matter more to be pitied than ours; and therefore, for God's sake, be good to us, for in you is all our trust.

And I beseech you, good master secretary, pray my lord my father and my lady be so good to us, and to let me have their blessings and my husband their good will; and I will never desire more of them. Also, I pray you, desire my lord of Norfolk and my lord my brother to be good to us. I dare not write to them, they are so cruel against us; but if, with any pain that I could take with my life, I might win their good wills, I promise you there is no child living would venture more than I. And so I pray you to report by me, and you shall find my writing true, and in all points which I may please them in I shall be ready to obey them nearest my husband, whom I am most bound

to; to whom I most heartily beseech you to be good unto, which, for my sake, is a poor banished man for an honest and godly cause. And seeing that I have read in old books that some, for as just causes, have by kings and queens been pardoned by the suit of good folks, I trust it shall be our chance, through your good help, to come to the same; as knoweth the (lord) God, who send you health and heart's ease. Scribbled with her ill hand, who is your poor, humble suitor, always to command,
Mary Stafford[7]

Katherine's mother, Mary, begged Cromwell to talk to the King on her behalf and through him perhaps the relationship with her sister could be improved. From the tone of the letter, Mary felt she had more chance of the King receiving her back into favour than she did from any of her family. Mary may never have returned to her sister's favour as she is not mentioned in court records after this time although Roldolfo Pio, the Papal Nuncio in Paris, placed her back at court to attend Anne in her final pregnancy or as he put it 'to keep up the deceit'. He believed that Anne had conjured up a pregnancy to keep herself in the King's good books and that Mary as her closest companion and sister helped her in keeping the rumours alive thus prolonging her ultimate downfall. But Mary was not close to her sister at this time and probably never saw her again after being sent from court. Anne truly had been pregnant and she gave birth to a stillborn son in January 1536. The miscarriage happened on the same day as Queen Catherine died but was said to have been caused by her finding the King entertaining Jane Seymour and more specifically her sitting on the king's lap. Distraught and upset, Anne lost her child that same evening. If he had lived, if she had given Henry his longed for son, her life would have been different. As it was Henry had had enough and had found her replacement. As for Anne, her life was now in danger, although she was yet to realise it.

When Queen Catherine died, there was still the pretence that Anne was in favour. King Henry exclaimed 'Thank god, now we are free from any fear of war!' when he heard the news of Queen Catherine's death and ordered celebrations to be held with Queen Anne in attendance. The Lady Mary was kept away from court while Princess Elizabeth was paraded in front of the gathered ladies and gentlemen as Henry underlined who his legitimate daughter now was.

Anne made some attempt to befriend Mary at this stage perhaps being sympathetic to her losing her mother - a guilty conscience goading her to try to make amends - but Mary would have none of it. Mary refused to accept Anne as Queen and who can blame her? She was in mourning for the mother that she had been kept away from, that she hardly ever saw and the blame was laid at Anne's door. Anne's patience wore thin and she wrote to Lady Shelton concerning Mary's attitude:

Mrs Shelton, my pleasure is that you do not further move the Lady Mary to be towards the King's Grace otherwise than it pleases herself. What I have done has been more for charity than for anything the king or I care what road she takes, or whether she will change her purpose, for if I have a son, as I hope shortly, I know what will happen to her; and therefore, considering the word of God, to do good to one's enemy, I wished to warn her beforehand, because I have daily experience that the king's wisdom is such as not to esteem her repentance of her rudeness and unnatural obstinacy when she has no choice. By the law of God and the king, she ought clearly to acknowledge her error and evil conscience if blind affection had not so blinded her eyes that she will see nothing but what pleases herself. Mrs Shelton, I beg you not to think to do me any pleasure by turning her from any of her wilful courses, because she could not do me good or evil; and do your duty according to the king's command, as I am assured you do.[8]

But Anne was soon to have other concerns. The same Cromwell who Mary Boleyn had beseeched to speak on her behalf was instrumental in the Queen's downfall. The king was looking for a way out of his marriage and Cromwell presented him with the ultimate solution. If Anne was accused of plotting the death of the King, it would be seen as high treason and warranted the death penalty. Why did Henry want to go to such extremes? Could he not have just divorced her? Back when the couple had been courting, Henry had made Anne the Marquess of Pembroke, this gave her power and prestige in her own right, a substantial yearly income and lands. He had given her the title primarily to elevate her status before their trip to France and her meeting with Francois I. If she was to become a Queen of England she had to be seen to be worthy of the King and only a woman of status could meet with the ladies of the French court. Her status gave her rights and he wanted no ex-wife to be in such a powerful position when he put her aside. Beheading was the easiest answer. He would have no scorned wife waiting in the shadows plotting against him. He had always feared that his treatment of Queen Catherine would result in a war with Spain. Catherine had many loyal supporters and Henry had no wish to have yet another wife conspiring against him with her allies once their marriage was annulled. Killing the Queen was the best solution and a way to erase her from his life. Henry was well aware that people thought Anne had bewitched him and turned him into a cuckolded husband. His embarrassment could be ended with the swing of a sword.

Cromwell compiled evidence against Anne that accused her of adultery with Mark Smeaton, her musician, Sir Henry Norris, a groom of the King's, William Brereton, another King's man, Sir Francis Weston and her own brother, George, Lord Rochford as well as conspiracy to murder the king. Two other men, Sir Thomas Wyatt and Sir Richard Page were also arrested but released without charge. Mark Smeaton was the only one of the men to confess his guilt but this had surely been due to the torture he endured.

On the 2nd May 1536 Anne was escorted to the Tower of London and placed in the care of the Constable of the Tower, Sir William Kingston. She was conducted to the Queen's lodgings and left in the company of her attendants. On the 12th, Norris, Brereton, Smeaton and Weston were condemned to be drawn, hanged, castrated and quartered by Lord Chancellor Audley. George was to be tried separately due to his position and status. Tellingly the King dismissed Anne's servants from her household in Greenwich at this time. Anne was never going to return home.

Anne was tried before hundreds of spectators. She sat dignified throughout her trial and refuted all charges put to her. But the King had already decided and the trial was merely a formality. Twenty six peers of the realm found her guilty and it was her uncle the Duke of Norfolk who read out:

Because thou hast offended our sovereign lord the King's Grace in committing treason against his person, the law of the realm is this: that thou shall be burnt here within the Tower of London on the Green, else to have thy head smitten off, as the King's pleasure shall be further known of the same.

On the 17th her brother George and the other men who were accused of adultery with the queen were beheaded on Tower Hill. Anne was executed two days later in the early hours of 19th May 1536. A swordsman from Calais (or St Omer, as a letter written by Mary of Hungary attests) was specifically employed to put an end to this Queen's life. Some historians believe Katherine was in attendance and witnessed her aunt's execution. Did Katherine really see her die? She would only have been about twelve at the time. There are no records of her being one of Anne's four ladies who accompanied her in the Tower but could her mother have sent her to be a companion to Anne in her final days? In an official guide to Westminster Abbey written in 1878, the author, Augustus Hale, presumes Katherine to have been there but she is not mentioned in any correspondence or writing of the times. The king had in fact chosen women to attend her aunt Anne that were not her close companions and could be relied on to be impartial and to report on Anne's behaviour. These included her aunts, Elizabeth Boleyn and Lady Shelton, Lady Kingston, Mrs Cosyn and Mrs Stonor but some of the women were family and as family Katherine may have been sent to Anne to comfort her in her last hours.

Katherine may not have been present to see her aunt die but she would surely have heard of her dying words or read of them. Anne left this world with dignity even though she had been accused of acts she did not commit. On the scaffold, she said:

Good Christian people! I am come hither to die, for according to the law, and by the law, I am judged to death; and therefore I will speak nothing against it. I come hither to accuse no man, nor to speak any thing of that whereof I am accused and condemned to die; but I pray God save the king, and send him long to reign over you, for a gentler, or a more merciful prince was there never; and to me he was ever a good, a gentle, and a sovereign lord. And if any person will meddle with my cause, I require them to judge the best. And thus I take my leave of the world, and of you all, and I heartily desire you all to pray for me. O Lord have mercy on me! To God I commend my soul.

There is such controversy over why Anne did not speak out against the King if she truly was innocent. For five men including her brother to have had relations with her seems implausible but maybe there was guilt in some part. Anne had known that her downfall was coming and she may have tried to stop its progress by becoming pregnant by one of her male companions.

But she may also have been kept from denouncing the King

and protesting her innocence because she wanted to keep Elizabeth safe. Elizabeth was her pride and joy and she demonstrated much affection for her. Before Anne's execution, her marriage was declared null and void making the Princess Elizabeth a bastard also. It is rumoured that the grounds on which the marriage was declared invalid again mentioned Katherine's mother, Mary and her relationship with the King. The Succession Act of 1536 would put into law that any children from Henry and Jane Seymour's marriage would be the King's legitimate heirs or failing that that he would write in his will who the next ruler after him would be - Mary and Elizabeth were now his illegitimate daughters and were effectively written out of the succession. Katherine would never have featured into King Henry's plans - she was irrelevant as the daughter of his mistress as now were his daughters from his previous marriage.

This child, Elizabeth, left without her mother and ignored by her father, was to grow up to be Queen against the odds and become Katherine's dearest friend, employer and early playmate.

Chapter Three

Growing Up with Elizabeth and Mary

After Queen Anne's death, Elizabeth was forgotten for a time and Lady Bryan had to write to Cromwell. The letter gives us great insight into how the household and Elizabeth was faring after her mother's death. Lady Bryan tells it like it is, so much so, that Cromwell added a note saying 'Apologises for her boldness in writing thus.'

...When your lordship was last here you bade me not mistrust the King or you, which gave me great comfort, and encourages me now to show you my poor mind. When my lady Mary was born the King appointed me lady Mistress, and made me a baroness; "And so I have been a m[other] to the children his Grace have had since." Now, as my lady Elizabeth is put from that degree she was in, and what degree she is at now I know not but by hearsay, I know not how to order her or myself, or her women or grooms. I beg you to be good lord to her and hers, and that she may have raiment, for she has neither gown nor kirtle nor petticoat, nor linen for smocks, nor kerchiefs, sleeves, rails, bodystychets, handkerchiefs, mufflers, nor "begens." "All thys har Graces mostake I have dreven of as long as I can, that, be my trothe, I cannot drive it no lenger."

Mr. Shelton says he is master of this house. "What fashion that shal be I cannot tel, for I have not sen it afore." I trust to your lordship, who, as every man reports, loveth honor, to see this house honorably ordered, "howsom ever it hath been aforetime." If the head of [the same] know what honor meaneth it will be the better ordered; if not, it will be hard to bring it to pass. Mr. Shelton would have my lady Elizabeth to dine and sup every day at the board of estate. It is not meet for a child of her age to keep such rule. If she do, I dare not take it upon me to keep her Grace in health; for she will see divers meats, fruits, and wine, that it will be hard for me to refrain her from. "Ye know, my lord, there is no place of correction there; and she is too young to correct greatly." I beg she may have a good mess of meat to her own lodging, with a good dish or two meet for her to eat of; and the reversion of the mess shall satisfy her women, a gentleman usher, and a groom; "which been eleven persons on her side." This will also be more economical.

My lady has great pain with her teeth, which come very slowly. This makes me give her her own way more than I would. "I trust to God and her teeth were well graft to have her Grace after another fashion than she is yet; so, as I trust, the King's Grace shall have great comfort in her Grace. For she is as toward a child and as gentle of conditions as ever I knew any in my life, Jesu preserve her Grace. As for a day or two at a hey time or whansomever it shall please the King's Grace to have her set abroad, I trust so to endeavour me that she shall so do as shall be to the King's honor and hers; and then after to take her ease again. I think Mr. Shelton will not be content with this. He may not know it is my desire, but that it is the King's pleasure and yours it should be so."

From Hunsdon with the evil hand of your daily bede woman.[1]

Katherine sympathised with the two girls that she spent her days with. As Katherine reached her twelfth birthday, Elizabeth was three while Mary was twenty. While Elizabeth was kept in the dark about the execution of her mother, Mary was well aware of her mother's death at the cold and forbidding castle of Kimbolton. The atmosphere in the nursery was surely charged with the emotions of the usurped Princess and the servants who tried to keep Elizabeth from knowing the truth about what had happened to Queen Anne.

Katherine herself had said goodbye to her mother two years before when she left court. Mary Boleyn had followed the example Mary Tudor had set and married a man for love. In the previous chapter, we saw how Katherine's mother had remarried in 1534 and it had caused a scandal. Mary had met William Stafford on a trip to Calais when she had accompanied her sister, Anne and the King. When Mary was sent from court in disgrace, she probably returned with him to Calais. Mary was gone from court and England, leaving her two children behind. Her younger son, Henry, was a ward of the court while Katherine remained in Elizabeth's household.

Elizabeth and Mary were now both declared bastards and Katherine joined their ranks for a time as just another daughter of Henry's. Elizabeth seems to have taken the change to her status in her stride although at such a young age, she would have little concept of what this would mean to her. She is often reported to have said to John Shelton 'how hath it, yesterday Lady Princess, and today but Lady Elizabeth?' Henry's fondness for his daughters rose and fell with his moods and his marital situation. He showed little affection to any of them and Katherine even less. His treatment of them prompted Mary at least to rethink her relationship to her sister. Mary began to treat Elizabeth with more affection and although there was still a shadow of mourning over their household, the girls began to warm to each other. For Mary, there was no longer any point in having tantrums over Elizabeth when she had been reduced to the same status as herself.

Their father had already been wooing a new lover before Anne's death and he spared no time in making their betrothal permanent. King Henry and his new Queen, Jane Seymour, were married on the 30th May 1536 in the Queen's Closet at York Place by Archbishop Cranmer, just 11 days after Anne had been beheaded. It was a quiet affair coming so soon after Anne's death. Henry had chosen a woman that could never remind him of his previous wife. Jane was everything Anne wasn't. She was plain, of average height and her appearance prompted Chapuys to comment that 'nobody thinks she has much beauty'. She was submissive and well-groomed by the Seymour family to become a compliant Queen. Jane was a peaceable Queen, one that didn't inflame Henry's temper, unlike Anne. Her motto, *bound to obey and serve*, says it all.

Henry kept Jane away from public scrutiny until June when he ceremoniously accompanied her from Greenwich to Whitehall by barge. The people of England who had not welcomed Anne to the throne were more accommodating of Jane and they lined the river to watch the new Queen sail past with their now thrice-married King.

The nursery household now changed under the reign of another Queen. Elizabeth was disregarded as her mother's daughter - Henry wanted no reminder of the mess his previous marriage had caused - but Mary was beginning to find more favour at court. Jane had been a firm supporter of her mother, Catherine of Aragon, and she upheld those traditional religious beliefs that the Queen had held so dear. She wanted Mary to regain the king's favour and pushed him to allow her back to court. But Henry was still incensed by his daughter's stubbornness. During the time of his divorce from her mother, Mary had refused to acknowledge her father as the Supreme Head of the Church of England and she would not agree that his marriage to her mother had been unlawful. Henry became so angry that he considered trying Mary for treason. Jane tried to intervene but this made Henry even angrier. Days passed where Mary tried to engage her father in discussion by writing to him and assuring him of her loyalty but he refused to answer her letters. She was told that unless she signed a paper of submission agreeing he was the Head of the Church, she was placing herself in great danger. Mary held out for as long as she could but eventually she signed the document agreeing to everything that she was against. She had been worn down and in fear of her life. There was nothing else she could do.

And the change was almost immediate. Henry was delighted that Mary had finally succumbed to his will and he began discussing her return to court. Jane couldn't have been happier. She wanted Mary to attend her and to take her place as Henry's daughter and her companion. Jane's brother was dispatched to present her with a new horse and to arrange her court wardrobe, preparing ahead for her triumphant return. Mary was delighted and wrote to Cromwell:

After my most hearty commendations, it is so long since I heard from the King my father that I am bold to send my servant, the bearer, with letters to the King and Queen to know how they do. If I have sent too soon molesting his Grace with my rude letters, please make my excuse. Till he shall licence me to come to his presence my comfort is to hear often of his health. My lord, your servant hath brought me the well favored horse that you have given me, with a very goodly saddle, for the which I do thank you with all my heart. I trust the riding upon him shall do my health much good, for I am wont to find great ease in riding. Your benefits increase daily towards me'.[2]

When finally Mary met with her father again, it had been six years since she had been in his presence. Jane took on the role of step-mother to Mary now Henry had warmed again to his eldest daughter. She was allowed her place at court even though she was not restored as Princess and she struck up a friendship with Jane that appears to have been mutual and pleasant for them both. But what about Elizabeth? Jane made no overt moves to include Elizabeth in court life or help her regain her father's favour. She was still young and perhaps Jane saw little point in making a fuss over her. Her mother's death and disgrace were still too raw to have the little girl at court, a reminder of the past queen, and Jane would only have incurred Henry's wrath if she had pressed him to be more attentive to the girl.

Mary had softened though and even began to buy Elizabeth small gifts and send them to her at Hatfield, visiting when she could. In July of 1536, Mary had written to her father concerning Elizabeth 'and such a child toward, as I doubt not but your Highness shall have cause to rejoice of in time coming; as knoweth Almighty God, who send your Grace, with the Queen my good mother, health, with the accomplishment of your desires.'[3] Not only was Mary warming to Elizabeth but she had wholly accepted Jane as her new mother.

Jane's peaceful nature had calmed the relationship between the girls and Mary's troubled behaviour was soothed so that the nursery became a place of tranquillity again and Elizabeth and Katherine could continue growing up as young girls do. It was a short-lived peace. The girls would be attending Queen Jane's funeral the very next year but before then there was a new addition to the family, born on 12th October 1537, their half-brother, Edward, the future King. Henry finally had the son that he had been waiting for and he was overjoyed. Bells rang across London, choirs sang, the celebrations were copious and the people rejoiced to have a male heir to Henry's throne at last.

Mary had already been with Queen Jane throughout the later stages of pregnancy and her labour at Hampton Court Palace. Elizabeth was allowed to visit them after Edward's birth and they both attended their brother's christening three days later. Katherine would probably have stayed at Hatfield although she may have been in Elizabeth's retinue. Mary acted as Edward's godmother while Elizabeth carried his heavily embroidered baptismal cloth or chrisom although she too was being carried, by Edward Seymour, the newly-created Viscount Beauchamp. Jane, like other new mothers, did not attend the christening but dressed in velvet and furs and sat waiting on a day bed in her chamber to receive the christening guests. Three days later, she collapsed, exhausted by a labour that had lasted three days and from which she would never recover.

Edward's birth was bittersweet. When Jane Seymour died of puerperal fever just twelve days after he came into the world,

Henry had lost a wife that he had, for once, been happy with. No-one had expected to lose the twenty-nine year old queen, least of all the king though we know that this was sadly often the case with many Tudor pregnancies. Some historians have suggested that she died of a caesarean birth but there is no evidence for this and she would hardly have been able to receive visitors after the christening had that been the case. This was not the time of safe surgical intervention. If a caesarean was performed in those days, it was fatal for the mother. Others thought that Jane's care had not been sufficient and that she had caught a chill but the most likely explanation is that she succumbed to childbed or puerperal fever caused by uterine infection after such a tough and prolonged labour.

The new Queen was gone after so short a reign. Henry shut himself away and mourned her passing. He had been happy to see Catherine and Anne meet their deaths but he had had such hopes for his latest Queen. However, she had done exactly what he wanted of her. She was the only Queen to have given him a son and for that, he mourned her all the harder.

Mary was chief mourner at her state funeral held on 12th November. As Jane's coffin was moved from Hampton Court to Windsor, Mary rode at the head of the procession on a horse draped in black velvet. She was buried in St George's Chapel, Windsor Castle - the only one of Henry's wives to be buried as Queen - and the Queen he would later join in her final resting place.

The household of girls, who had settled under Jane's calming influence, were joined by the motherless baby Edward. Change had once again come to the nursery and this time it was Elizabeth who was pushed aside. Lady Bryan now had to take charge of the new addition as she had done when Mary and Elizabeth were born and set up Prince Edward's household and daily routine. It was Kat Champernowne who was to take over Elizabeth's care. Kat had joined the household in 1536 but now took the position of governess to the young girl. The well-educated Kat became Elizabeth's tutor in her early days, teaching her languages, maths, history, geography and astronomy as well as more ladylike skills such as dancing, riding, needlework and embroidery. She became the mother that Elizabeth did not have, spending all her time on her young charge's education and deportment and in later years, Elizabeth would tell of her 'great labour and pain in bringing me up in learning and honesty'. We can imagine Katherine sitting in on their lessons, learning to read and write and also taking religious instruction. Katherine would grow up to be as protestant as Elizabeth while Mary was a firm Catholic, like her mother.

Education and religion were one and the same for Tudor women. Mary's first translation was of a Latin prayer while Elizabeth's was a translation of the work of Jean Calvin, a protestant theologian. This reflected the tutoring they received and set the tone for their later religious beliefs. Katherine too would hold strong religious beliefs that she later produced in writing. In Melissa Franklin-Harkrider's book , *Women, Reform and Community in Early Modern England*, she states 'Catherine Parr, Catherine Knollys, Elizabeth Tyrwhit and Elizabeth Vane all composed collections of psalms and meditations that exhorted other women to prayer and Bible study'. Katherine herself is credited with writing *A Heavenly Recreation or comforts to the sowle*, published posthumously by Richard Watkins around 1569.

This was a time when women weren't expected to learn much else; a time where they remained firmly in the background while their husbands ruled the roost. Girls in general were expected to learn how to maintain a household, look after their husbands, children and servants and to conduct themselves well in social situations. Social skills were paramount for girls who hoped to gain court positions. They should be able to engage in conversation, dance, play music and entertain guests with grace and femininity. But not all women conformed to the times and there are records of women like Margaret More, Thomas More's daughter, who challenged the norms and received an education that included theology, astronomy, languages and geometry as well as Elizabeth herself.

Both girls and boys were sent to grow up in other households. It was a type of social networking, giving the children the best chance in life of making contacts that would further their prospects. Like Katherine, there could be several children from different families all housed together attending on whichever lord and lady to further their education and for children from more well-to-do families, to increase their chances of rising to take a position at court. Not every child was taught to read or write although reading was a skill far common in Tudor times than writing was. Especially with girls, reading was encouraged so that they could read religious tracts, the Bible and books on good behaviour.

Kat taught Elizabeth as much as she could but Elizabeth was a fast learner. She went on to further her education with tutors such as Sir John Cheke and William Grindal. At no point did she receive the education her brother was receiving, an education that was preparing him for kingship. And Edward was thriving under Lady Bryan's care. She wrote to the King in 1539:

My lord Prince is in good health and merry. Would to God the King and your Lordship had seen him last night. The minstrels played, and his Grace danced and played so wantonly that he could not stand still, as Mr. Chamberlain and my lady his wife can show you.

Elizabeth was studious and intelligent, continuing her studies even after she was made Queen and had to learn a whole new role. Mary, on the other hand, would learn those ropes sooner and her reign would have a devastating effect on the population while Katherine, the unacknowledged daughter who could never aspire to such heights, was set to become a lady-in-waiting.

Elizabeth and Katherine had formed a friendship that was to last Katherine's lifetime but for now, Katherine's life was taking a different path and one that would lead her to Anne of Cleves.

Chapter Four

Maid of Honour

Katherine mourned her grandfather, Thomas Boleyn, at his passing in the March of 1539. He had been back at court after her aunt Anne's fall from grace and had been returned to the king's confidence once again. Henry also mourned his death and ordered masses to be said for his soul. Whatever their relationship had been in later years, Henry had executed both his son and daughter. It was the least he could do. Thomas was buried at St Peter's Church near the family home at Hever, where his tomb was decorated with a depictive brass showing him dressed as a Knight of the Garter with Anne's falcon crest appearing by his right shoulder. His death meant that Hever, the Boleyn family home, returned to the crown and Katherine's mother, Mary, might return to England to claim her part of the inheritance.

This was a year of change for Katherine. Elizabeth was growing into an intelligent Queen-to-be and Katherine was now fifteen, the right age to leave her childhood days behind and to take her first court position, that of maid of honour to Henry's new wife, Anne of Cleves. Henry had finally begun looking for a new Queen and had asked the king of France to line up a bevy of beauties so that he might inspect them and choose his new bride. King François was shocked at his proposal. Henry had become notorious for the way he treated his wives and the ladies of the French court were in no rush to become the next Queen of England. The search for a new bride had to reach further afield and, after being presented with miniatures of the Duke of Cleve's two sisters who were living in Germany, Henry's next wife was selected.

In December of 1539, Anne of Cleves arrived in England at

Deal in Kent after months of negotiation and Katherine was ready and waiting to join her entourage. There had been no Queen for several years and no ladies-in-waiting so when it was announced that Henry was to marry again, the ladies of the Tudor court clamoured for a position with the new Queen. To become a maid of honour was honour indeed and Katherine was shown favouritism in gaining this appointment, another indicator that Henry was looking out for her even though he would never acknowledge her. Katherine was finally to enter the world into which by dint of her birth she had been refused so far.

Plans were put in place to ensure that Anne was well treated and welcomed to her new country and home. In a list entitled 'For the Reception of Anne of Cleves' the details were set out:

1. The lord Deputy and Council of Calais, with the men of arms and such of the retinue as they and the lord Admiral shall appoint, shall receive her at her entry into the English Pale, and after due saluta-tions conduct her and her train into the town. 2. About St. Peter's without Calais, the said lord Admiral and those assigned to keep him company shall meet her and in like manner wait upon her into the town to her lodging. 3. On her arrival at Dover the duke of Suffolk and lord Warden of the Cinque Ports, with the other lords appointed to wait upon them, and the duchess of Suffolk and other ladies, shall receive her at her landing, and convey her to the castle, attend upon her during her abode there, and at her departure conduct her to Canterbury, and so forth till her meeting with the King. 4. The archbishop of Canterbury, with certain other bps. and gentlemen, are to meet her beyond Canterbury and convey her to her lodging there, and in like manner attend upon her till her meeting with the King. 5. She shall be met on the down beyond Rochester by the duke of Norfolk and certain other lords and gentlemen, who shall likewise wait upon her till she come to the King's presence. 6. On this side Derford the earl of Rutland, who is to be her lord chamberlain, Sir Thos Denys, chancellor, Sir Edw. Baynton, vice-chamberlain, Sir

John Dudley, master of her horse, and all others appointed to be of her Council, and also the lady Margaret Douglas, the duchess of Richmond, and other ladies which shall be her "ordinary waiters," 30 in all, shall meet her, and be presented, by the abp. of Canterbury, and the dukes of Norfolk and Suffolk, as her own train and household, and so wait upon her till she approach the King's presence, when all the yeomen and meaner sort shall avoid. 7. On the hill_there shall be "pight" the King's rich pavilion, and others for other noble personages to retire to after she shall be presented to His Highness, and there shall be prepared wine, fruits, and spices, in manner of a banquet. 8. Before the King meets with her, all serving men shall depart and range themselves aloof in the field. The rest of the gentlemen to ride in two wide ranges on either side that His Majesty may have only such as shall be assigned before and after him, &c. 9. The duke of Norfolk, being Earl Marshal, shall appoint persons with tipped staves to keep the streets between the town's end and the gate of Greenwich, the way whereunto shall pass about the park and through the town to the door directly against the west end and the late Friars church, and so to the great gate on the water side at Greenwich. The said door leading out of the lane where the stables be into the church of the late Friars, and all other strait places, to be enlarged. The streets to be gravelled, paved, made clean, and put in as good order as may be; barriers to be made all along the Thames side, that no man be in danger of drowning by press of people. The charge of this to be committed to Nedam, the King's carpenter. 10. Every lord and gentleman is to alight out of the way without the said gate and go on foot to the Court. Only the King, the Queen, and the ladies to ride into the Court. 11. When the King shall be in his pavilion, the Vice-Chamberlain with the Guard shall repair to Greenwich, and place the said Guard in such parts of the house as shall be meet to keep order. 12. When the King leaves the pavilion for Greenwich, all gentlemen not named in a special list to ride before him, shall stand on the heath in two ranges for his Grace and train to pass. 13. The mayor of London with all the aldermen and crafts shall be upon the Thames, in barges well apparelled and furnished with as many kinds of music as they can get, to congratulate her arrival, but none of them shall set foot on land. The Knight Marshal, or some other, should appoint the place where every barge shall lie. 14. The chief officers of the Household are to furnish the hall, the porters to be at the gate, &c.[1]

Several ladies met Anne as she set foot on English soil including the Duchess of Suffolk and the Ladies Cobham, Hart, Haulte, Finche and Hales while Katherine stayed with the other five maids of honour to ready the queen's chambers at court. Anne Bassett, Dorothy Bray, Catherine Howard, Mary Norris and Ursula Stourton had been lucky enough to also gain the positions of maids of honour and they were presided over by other great ladies of the court and the privy chamber including Mary Arundell, Countess of Sussex, Frances Brandon, Marchioness of Dorset, Lady Margaret Douglas, the Duchess of Richmond, the Countess of Rutland and Lady Dudley. Katherine had barely known her uncle George, the brother of her mother Mary and aunt Anne but she was also joined in the new Queen's household by the deceased George's wife, Lady Rochford. All the women eagerly anticipated the arrival of the new queen-to-be and their new lives attending on her at court.

There was someone else who was arriving in England along with the queen. Someone who was important to Katherine, someone she had not seen for several years - her mother. Mary Boleyn had returned with her husband, William Stafford, who had been attending the Lord Admiral, Sir William Fitzwilliam, in France. Both Katherine's mother and step-father had been a part of the reception committee that met Anne in Calais. As Anne had inspected the king's ships, William had accompanied the Admiral and he and his wife had both attended the banquets and celebrations that were held in Anne's honour before she set sail for England.

Anne of Cleves was officially greeted at Dover and then continued to Rochester Castle as per the well thought out plan. It was here that Henry tried to play a courtly game of appearing before his bride-to-be dressed as an ordinary man. He strode into her apartments with five of his men and tried to capture her attention. The whole point was for her to recognise him for her king and new husband, being swept away by his handsomeness and stature. But Anne looked at the strange crowd of men that had burst into her rooms and she wondered what on earth was going on. She neither recognised the king nor thought much of the game which prompted Henry to turn to Cromwell and declare 'I like her not'.

However, Chapuys for once, wrote of the incident as having a happy outcome:

And on New Year's Day in the afternoon the king's grace with five of his privy chamber, being disguised with mottled cloaks with hoods so that they should not be recognized, came secretly to Rochester, and so went up into the chamber where the said Lady Anne was looking out of a window to see the bull-baiting which was going on in the courtyard, and suddenly he embraced and kissed her, and showed here a token which the king had sent her for New Year's gift, and she being abashed and not knowing who it was thanked him, and so he spoke with her. But she regarded him little, but always looked out the window.... and when the king saw that she took so little notice of his coming he went into another chamber and took off his cloak and came in again in a coat of purple velvet. And when the lords and knights saw his grace they did him reverence.... and then her grace humbled herself lowly to the king's majesty, and his grace saluted her again, and they talked together lovingly, and afterwards he took her by the hand and led her to another chamber where their graces amused themselves that night and on Friday until the afternoon.'

Now in his late forties, Henry was ageing by the standards of the times. He was troubled by his leg and often succumbed to fits of temper brought on by ill-health and the stresses and strains of controlling his kingdom. Anne had slighted Henry from the very beginning and he found her repulsive. He undertook the pleasantries that she deserved by virtue of her status but he was not impressed by what he saw. He hated the way she dressed, being in the German fashion. He hated the way she looked, he hated her mannerisms and the fact that she only spoke German. She couldn't even play an instrument or sing a tune to please him. He treated her well but was furious that his ambassadors had spoken of her attractiveness which he failed to see and was enraged that the portraits he had been shown painted her in a far more attractive light than she was in reality. He found her distasteful but continued with the marriage, fearful of upsetting the alliance he had made with the German duchies. Whether he liked her or not, the court had come alive again with young women to fill the new Queen's household and it would not be long before his eye wandered to someone who he found much more pleasing.

Katherine saw her mother again for the first time in years as she met Anne of Cleves and joined her household. It was a time of celebration and joy for her. And it was the start of something new and someone special in her life. While her father had begun looking for someone more comely to share his bed, Katherine was feeling her own stirrings of attraction. In the king's retinue was a dark-haired, handsome young man who was to play a major part in Katherine's life - Francis Knollys.

But for now there was a royal wedding to prepare for. The wedding of King Henry VIII and his fourth bride, Anne of Cleves, was held on the Feast of the Epiphany, 6th January 1540, and Archbishop Cranmer once again conducted the proceedings. Henry was increasingly unhappy with his choice of bride complaining, 'if it were not to satisfy the world and my realm, I would not do that I must do this day, ay for none earthly thing.'

But still he dressed in a 'gowne of clothe of gold, raised with flowers of sylver, furred with black jenettes, his cote crimosyn sattyn all to cutte and embroidered and tied with great diamonds, and a ryche coller about his necke'[2] to impress his new wife and his court. Katherine helped Anne into the wedding dress she had brought with her from Germany which was also designed to show the new queen in all her splendour. She wore 'a gowne of ryche cloth of gold set full of large flowers of great and orient pearle, made after the Dutch fassion rownde, her here hangyng downe, whiche was faire, yellow and long. On her head a coronal of gold replenished with great stone, and set about full of braunches of rosemary, about her necke and middle, juelles of great valew and estimacion'.[3]

After the wedding ceremony, the rest of the day passed with prayer and a sumptuous dinner followed by more 'bankettes, maskes and diverse dysportes, tyll the tyme came that it pleased the kyng and her to take their rest'[4]. Henry, the unwilling bridegroom, joined Anne in their marriage bed with a heavy heart. Anne was anxious enough and so concerned with what the night might bring that she did not notice the King's reluctance. The events of their wedding night were reported to Cromwell the next day and Henry was not pleased. When Cromwell asked the King how he liked the Queen, he erupted with anger and spat out 'I liked her before not well, but now I like her much worse! She is nothing fair, and have evil smells about her. I took her to be no maid by reason of the looseness of her breasts and other tokens, which, when I felt them, strake me so to the heart, that I had neither will nor courage to prove the rest. I can have no appetite for displeasant airs. I have left her as good a maid as I found her'.[5] If Anne had known that not only did he think her unattractive but that he also thought she smelt pungently, she would have been ashamed and embarrassed but Henry had conducted himself well and Anne was none the wiser.

And things still did not improve after the wedding. Henry's

pride and more importantly his sex life was suffering. He just couldn't bring himself to sleep with Anne, even if it was his duty and his only way of producing more heirs to the throne. 'Her body (was) in such a sort disordered and indisposed... (it could not) excite and provoke any lust in him'[6].

But Anne still seems to have been oblivious to Henry's plight. Katherine was as amazed as Anne's other maids at her lack of understanding about her marital duties. It has been reported that she told them 'When he comes to bed, he kisses me and taketh me by the hand and biddeth me "Goodnight, sweetheart" and in the morning kisses me and biddeth me, "Farewell, darling". Is this not enough?'[7]. To which Lady Rutland was said to reply, 'Madam, there must be more than this, or it will be long ere we have a Duke of York, which all this realm most desireth'.[8]

Henry hadn't had any problems before with women of his choosing as far as we know. He insisted that he thought himself 'able to do the act with other but not with her'. Anne just didn't do it for him and he consulted with his doctors, Chambers and Butts, about the matter. Dr Chamber advised him that if he couldn't be 'provoked or stirred in that act' then he shouldn't enforce it.[9]

Henry's pattern of having affairs with his Queen's ladies-in-waiting or picking his new Queen from amongst them was to repeat itself. There was the hint of rumour and romance in the air but it definitely wasn't with his new wife. Henry had given Anne Bassett, one of Katherine's companions, a horse and saddle, showing his favour and sparking the suggestion that Anne was something more than just a maid of honour to the Queen. But it was Catherine Howard who had really taken his fancy. Henry visited the ladies often to see his new fancy, under the pretence of seeing the Queen. Katherine would have seen a lot of her father in the days that he spent with them and she may not have been happy with what she was witnessing.

In April of 1540, Catherine Howard was granted lands around

the same time as Katherine's mother was allowed her Boleyn inheritance. The King granted 'William Stafford and Mary, his wife, livery of lands, the said Mary being daughter and heir of Thomas, late Earl of Wiltshire and Ormond...the manors of Southt, alias Southtboram and Henden in Henden Park, and all lands in Hever and Brasted, Kent, which belonged to the said Earl'.[10] Whereas Mary was due her inheritance through her father's death, Catherine was being given gifts and land as Henry's new mistress.

May was a momentous time for Katherine and she had little time to spend on court rumour. At just sixteen years of age she married Francis Knollys, the handsome young man she had met the previous year, a twenty-six year old member of Henry's household. Tudor women were often betrothed at an early age but to marry so young was unusual. Perhaps Henry had acted in her fatherly interests and had arranged this match. It doesn't appear that he gave gifts or any sum of money at their wedding but he did make sure that the Knollys manor of Rotherfield Greys near Henley in Oxfordshire was passed to them.

On 10th June 1540, the court was once again abuzz with rumour but this time it wasn't romance that was in the air but the news of the fall of one of Henry's closest confidants. Henry could never forgive Thomas Cromwell for arranging his marriage to Anne of Cleves despite all his years of working to ensure Henry's happiness and the smooth running of his kingdom. Henry was done with the pretence of his marriage. He wanted Anne gone and Catherine Howard to replace her. And Cromwell would suffer the consequences.

Cromwell knew that he was in trouble. As he left parliament to attend a dinner, a gust of wind blew off his hat. It was typical for gentlemen watching to remove theirs also as a mark of respect but Cromwell was ignored and still no one spoke to him as they dined together. At the meeting of the council that followed when he went to take his place at the table, the Duke of

Norfolk shouted to him, 'Cromwell, do not sit there; that is no place for thee. Traitors do not sit amongst gentlemen'. As Cromwell replied, 'I am not a traitor', he was arrested by the Captain of the Guard and escorted to the Tower. Although they had not told him, Cromwell had been arrested for treason.

When Anne of Cleves heard of Cromwell's arrest, she began to worry for her own safety. On 24th June, she was told to relocate to Richmond to a beautiful red bricked palace, of which little remains, on the edge of the River Thames and close to a deer park and hunting grounds. She was originally told it was for the benefit of her health and would remove her from the risk of catching the plague but her suspicions were growing. As she talked to her ladies, Katherine amongst them, the gossip turned to Catherine Howard. Anne had heard the rumours about the King and Catherine and had seen her flirtatiousness with her own eyes but what would this mean for her? Anne settled into an anxious routine until 6th July when the King's men arrived to discuss her marriage to the king. They had been charged with getting Anne's consent to an investigation into the validity of their marriage. Henry was up to his old tricks, trying to find a way to rid himself of the Queen he had never desired. And once again he turned to God as being the judge of his actions.

Henry summoned the leading clergymen of the country to examine the issues and evidence surrounding his marriage. Three arguments were put forward for its annulment. The first pointed to Anne's previous betrothal to the Duke of Lorraine's son, the Marquis of Pont-à-Mousson, even though this had been renounced in 1535. The argument ran that the notarial certificate that had been supplied was not legal document enough and the betrothal was still outstanding. The second argument was Henry's lack of consent to the marriage which he showed evidence of in his own words and that of others and the third and final argument, and one that must have shamed Anne, was the marriage's lack of consummation. It was a done deal and the gathered clergy agreed to the annulment.

Henry had got his way again but at least Anne did not lose her head. She was told of the verdict and agreed it was right. Again Henry had left a woman with no choice. Anne knew that if she put up any resistance her life would be in danger. Agreeing with the king was the best course of action. She wrote to Henry:

It may please you majesty to know that, though this case must needs be most hard and sorrowful unto me, for the great love which I bear to your most noble person, yet, having more regard to God and his trust than to worldly affection, as it beseemed me, at the beginning, to submit me to such examination and determination of the said clergy, whom I have and do accept for judges competent in that behalf. So now being ascertained how the same clergy hath therein given their judgement and sentence, I knowledge myself hereby to accept and approve the same, wholly and entirely putting myself, for my state and condition, to your highness' goodness and pleasure; most humbly beseeching your Majesty that, though it be determined that the pretended matrimony between us is void and of none effect, whereby I neither can nor will repute myself your Grace's wife, considering this sentence (whereunto I stand) and your Majesty's clean and pure living with me, yet it will please you to take me for one of your most humble servants, and so determine of me, as I may sometimes have the fruition of your most noble presence; which as I shall esteem for a great benefit, so, my lords and others of your Majesty's council, now being with me, have put me in comfort thereof; and that your highness will take me for your sister; for the which I most humbly thank you accordingly. [11]

This pliable, easy-going Queen accepted her demotion to being known as Henry's sister with a sigh of relief and decided to make the most of living in England with an income of five hundred pounds a year, the use of two royal houses and precedence over all women except the new queen and the princesses. She may not have been able to return to her home in the Rhineland but she had escaped the fate of Henry's previous Queens and she could continue to live in some comfort for the rest of her days.

One of the residences she received as part of her annulment package was Hever Castle, Katherine's family home, and Katherine and her family were never to stay there again. It was time for Katherine to move on. Anne of Cleve's household was reduced and she was no longer needed as her maid of honour. Some historians believe that Katherine transferred to the new Queen's household. Katherine had become friends with Catherine Howard during the time they were serving Anne. Both similar in age, they had spent time together, and many days laughing and giggling at the foreign Queen's strange mannerisms and speech, so she may well have stayed at court to prepare Catherine for her new role as Queen although her stay would have been short. Katherine fell pregnant soon after her marriage to Francis and became a mother for the first time at the tender age of seventeen to Henry (Harry) Knollys, probably named affectionately after her father the King, in the Easter of 1541.

Whilst Katherine was away from court starting her new family, Henry was wooing the fifteen year old Catherine. He called her his 'blushing rose without a thorn'. She was young, beautiful, frivolous and exuberant; in complete comparison to Henry who daily suffered from his ulcerated leg and had gained a vast amount of weight in recent years. Perhaps that is why he became so besotted with her. She was beauty and all things youthful to his massive, ageing and ailing body. She was everything that reminded him of his glory days. She made him feel alive again.

Henry married Catherine Howard at Oatlands Palace in Weybridge, Surrey on the 28th July 1540. It was rumoured that Catherine was pregnant and this may have added to their haste but no child was forthcoming nor was there ever to be one. On the same day, Thomas Cromwell was led from his room in the

Tower to be executed for treason. How easy it was for Henry to rid himself of one of his most previously trusted men while at the same time taking yet another bride.

Although Henry thought that Catherine was his new prize, it wasn't long before being married to an overweight, increasingly cantankerous king bored her and she found new ways of amusing herself. Catherine had adopted the motto 'No other wish but his' but her own wishes were becoming more important. Here was a teenage girl for whom being a Queen was a novelty, an amusing escapade; full of dancing, music, jewels, dressing up and playing games.

She had no wish to take on the duties of a Queen or of a stepmother. Katherine may have been kept on as her maid of honour but Henry's youngest daughter and son would rarely have been seen. During this time Elizabeth was growing up away from court as was Edward but the Lady Mary was often in attendance. Mary's feelings for Catherine Howard matched those she had had for Anne Boleyn. Here was another woman related to the Boleyns that had gained the run of the court. Henry doted on his new wife, showering her with gifts and acquiescing to her very whim. Mary had no time for her. Not only was she older than her new step-mother but this Catherine was the antithesis of what she stood for.

Catherine had grown up in her grandmother's household where she had flirted and played with the attentions of the opposite sex. One of the men she had met here was Henry Manox who was employed to give music lessons to the girls in the Dowager Duchess of Norfolk's care. She tired of him when she met the dashing and handsome Francis Dereham and due to her grandmother's lax care she was able to do more with him than any respectable girl should.

Foolishly, when Catherine was made Queen she also made Francis Dereham her private secretary, bringing the past into her present. But her old suitors no longer had any real appeal for her other than being around to flatter and flirt with her. Catherine had taken a liking to one of the King's gentlemen of the privy chamber, Thomas Culpeper, who was also a distant cousin. She sent him gifts and little notes encouraging him and goading him on. When the King took her on his progress in the summer of 1541, she got Lady Rochford to smuggle Culpeper up to her rooms. She was the talk of the court and for good reason. The King was being made a fool of but who would tell him?

It fell to Cranmer, who fearing the King's reaction, slipped him a letter whilst he was at prayer in the chapel at Hampton Court Palace. Henry was furious but not with the Queen. He refused to believe what he saw as scandal and lies, demanding an inquiry to find the vicious rumour-monger and put a stop to the denunciation of his precious rose but Cranmer knew there was some truth in the accusations. He had talked to John Lascelles who had told him more about the improprieties of Catherine's past after hearing of them from his sister who had lived with her in the Duchess' house and he began compiling evidence against Catherine. When Cranmer interrogated her and questioned her actions, she wept and had hysterical fits but finally admitted to having slept with Dereham prior to her marriage with the King. Cranmer helped her to write her confession but she called him back wishing to change it and this time she made out that Dereham had taken her by force and that she had never consented to what passed between them. What she did say was damning enough, 'he hath lain with me, sometimes in his doublet and hose, and two or three times naked, but not so naked that he had nothing upon him, for he had always at the least his doublet, and as I do think his hose also; but I mean naked, when his hose was put down'.

Henry was given her confession as well as a letter pleading forgiveness. In it she said:

I, your Grace's most sorrowful subject and vile wretch in the world, not worthy to make any recommendations unto your Majesty, do only make my most humble submission and confession of my faults. And where no cause of mercy is given on my part, yet of your most accustomed mercy extended to all other men undeserved, most humbly on my hands and knees do desire one particle thereof to be extended unto me, although of all other creatures most unworthy either to be called your wife or subject. My sorrow I can by no writing express, nevertheless I trust your most benign nature will have some respect unto my youth, my ignorance, my frailness, my humble confession of my faults and plain declaration of the same, referring to me wholly unto your Grace's pity and mercy. First at the flattering and fair persuasions of Manox, being but a young girl I suffered him at sundry times to handle and touch the secret parts of my body...Also Francis Dereham by many persuasions procured me to his vicious purpose, and obtained first to lie upon my bed with his doublet and hose, and after within the bed, and finally he lay with me naked, and used me in such sort as a man doth his wife, many and sundry times...I was so desirous to be taken unto your Grace's favour, and so blinded with the desire of worldly glory, that I could not, nor had grace, to consider how great a fault it was to conceal my former faults from your Majesty, considering that I intended ever during my life to be faithful and true unto your Majesty after; nevertheless, the sorrow of mine offences was ever before mine eyes, considering the infinite goodness of your Majesty towards me from time to time ever increasing and not diminishing. Now I refer the judgement of all my offences with my life and death wholly unto your most benign and merciful Grace to be considered by no justice of your Majesty's laws but only by your infinite goodness, pity, compassion and mercy, without the which I acknowledge myself worthy of extreme punishment.[12]

Catherine had done a good job of admitting to her liaisons with Manox and Dereham, admitting her faults and begging for the King's mercy. Henry was appeased and many at court felt he may offer her forgiveness but Cranmer wasn't finished. In her confession, Catherine had also mentioned Culpeper but only that Dereham had asked her in a fit of jealousy if she would marry him. Cranmer was intrigued and investigated further, now paying heed to the rumours that had circulated the court earlier in the year. There was something about this Culpeper and his relationship with the Queen that Cranmer was driven to find out.

In a search of Culpeper's belongings, the most damning evidence was found. A letter from the Queen that hinted that their relationship had been a close one.

Master Culpeper
I heartily recommend me unto you, praying you to send me word how that you do. I did hear that ye were sick, and I never longed for anything so much as to see you. it maketh my heart to die when I do think that I cannot always be in your company. Come to me when Lady Rochford be here, for then I shall be best at leisure to be at your commandment...And thus I take my leave of you, trusting to see you shortly again. And I would you were with me now, that you might see what pain I take in writing to you.
Yours as long as life endures,
Katherine[13]

As well as confirming Cranmer's suspicions about the Queen, it prompted the interrogation of Lady Rochford for arranging the late night trysts between Catherine and Thomas and she told her interrogators everything. Although Culpeper never admitted to sleeping with Catherine, he did admit that he 'intended to do ill with her and likewise the Queen so minded to do with him' but that 'he had not passed beyond words'. Catherine also refused to admit that she had slept with Culpeper. They both knew their lives were on the line.

But it hardly mattered now. Cranmer had enough evidence to convict Culpeper and Catherine's previous lover, Dereham. Both

Dereham and Culpeper were tried together and the verdict was unanimous. They were to be drawn on hurdles to Tyburn where they would be hanged, drawn and quartered. Both men were executed on 10th December 1541 but Culpeper was allowed a final act of mercy. His sentence was reduced to beheading whereas Dereham underwent the whole sordid process that led to his death.

Catherine was waiting at Syon Abbey in Brentford for news of her own punishment during the next few weeks even though there could only be one outcome. On 10th February 1542, she was taken to the Tower and if there had been any doubt in her mind, she now knew that her time was short. This young girl who had so joyously played at being Queen had not taken her role seriously enough nor had she realised how her romantic liaisons would be her downfall. Henry would not stand to be taken for a fool, as much as he loved her.

Catherine Howard was executed on 13th February 1542. As she stood before the block she asked that 'all Christian people...take regard unto her worthy and just punishment with death'. Lady Rochford followed her and was executed with the same axe, fresh with Catherine's blood.

Katherine mourned the loss of the pretty vivacious Queen and her late uncle's wife but she had no time to dwell on it. With one son under a year old, she was now pregnant with her second child. Katherine had moved from childhood to a maid of honour to becoming a mother, and her family would be all important to her in the coming days.

Chapter Five

The Two Henrys

Katherine and her brother, Henry, lost their mother Mary in the July of 1543. It must have been a quiet funeral with no great tomb or plaque erected in her honour. In fact, her final resting place is something of a mystery with places like Hever Castle, Westminster Abbey and the church at Rochford all being put forward as her burial place. We will never know if King Henry mourned the passing of his previous mistress or if he even acknowledged that she was gone. Given that there are no records of her burial and nothing to mark her final resting place, it seems that Mary, once loved and adored before all others, was now a memory of the past.

Katherine attended the funeral service with her brother, Henry, whom she had seen little of while they were growing up. Henry's parentage is as much discussed as Katherine's and it was always believed that he was the elder child and therefore the King's but we now know that he was Mary's second child, born last, probably in 1526 although Weir has suggested that his birth date was actually in 1525. If this is the case it rules out that William Carey, Mary Boleyn's first husband, was paid off to keep quiet about his parentage. A grant was given to him two weeks before Henry's birth on the 4th March 1526 but if Henry had been born a year early then the grant does not correspond with his coming into the world. It is more probable that Mary's affair had finished with King Henry before little Henry was born. But it may have been that this pregnancy was the cause of the ending of their affair.

If Katherine was King Henry's unacknowledged child then so too might have been her brother, Henry. In 1531, a Venetian ambassador, Lodovico Falier, reported that 'The King has also a natural son, born to him of the widow of one of his peers; a youth of great promise, so much does he resemble his father'[1] and he may have been referring to Henry Carey, as his mother Mary was a widow by this time but so too was Elizabeth Blount, mother of Henry Fitzroy whom the king had acknowledged. Which Henry Falier was discussing is not clear.

As a toddler, Henry was made a ward of court after William Carey died of the sweating sickness and his aunt, Anne Boleyn, was given his wardship by the King. Anne was anxious to provide for Henry even though her relationship with her sister was on rocky ground and she arranged for him to be sent to a prestigious monastery for his education. Regardless of any family discord, Anne had a responsibility to the young Henry Carey and made sure that his education was a good one. Syon Abbey was in those days a monastery dedicated to the Bridgettine Order in Isleworth near Brentford, Middlesex. Established in 1415, Henry V had laid its first foundation stone. It was a place of learning with an immense library of over fourteen hundred books and was well known for the quality of its spiritual learning and the preachers who resided there. It was the obvious choice for starting a young child of the court on a learned path.

Catherine of Aragon had spent much time at Syon but its favour with the king subsided as did his affection for his wife. In later years, the abbey would be the target of King Henry's wrath. Richard Reynolds, confessor to the abbey's nuns, was executed in 1535 and his body was displayed at the gateway to Syon. He had refused to accept that the King was the new head of the Church of England and, like many others who came up against the king and his will, he paid the ultimate price. By 1539, Henry VIII had dissolved this most wealthy of monasteries and its inhabitants fled abroad to the Netherlands. Today little remains of the abbey at the current location of Syon Park and what is left of its collection of books resides with the University of Exeter. For

Henry though, his teachers at the abbey had provided an excellent start to his education.

Mr Skidmore, a priest at Syon Abbey, had seen Henry there and added to the rumours that he might be the King's son. The vicar of Isleworth, John Hale, who was vehemently against the Boleyns, also added to rumours about Henry but he was so anti-Boleyn we can hardly cite him as a credible witness. In the Letters and Papers, Foreign and Domestic of Henry VIII, Volume 8: January-July 1535, the discourse between Skidmore and Hale played out. One objection reads 'That Skydmore says Hale called the King the "Molywarppe" that Merlin prophesied of, that turned all up, and that the King was accursed of God's own mouth, and that the marriage between the King and Queen was unlawful'. There was obviously bad blood between them and Hale was forced to defend himself.

Hale told the Privy Council:

I fell and hurt my leg at Wyngham, at Allhallowtide was twelve-month, and remained till about Candlemas next. On Saturday after Ash Wednesday I fell into a fervent ague. How long I continued, with various relapses, the parishioners of Isleworth know, so that I took not my journey through whole five weeks before Michaelmas last, and lost "our Lady's quarter" ended the Midsummer before that by my sickness. I had several falls from my horse, from one of which I was troubled in my wits, as also by age and lack of memory. Will nevertheless report, as well as I can, with whom I talked, and in what manner, of the King's grace. I remember, about two years ago, the fellow of Bristow showed, both to me and others of Syon, the prophecies of Marlyon; for, by my truth, Master Skydmore showed me also the same, with whom I had several conversations concerning the King's marriage and other behaviours of his bodily lust. Once Cownsell the porter "sayd that our suffren had a short of maydons over oon of his chambyres at Farnam while he was with the oold lord of Wynchester." Had also conversations with Skydmore, with Sir

*Thomas my priest, and with Master Leeke; and once, I think, about
two years ago, of the Acts of Parliament made against churchmen,
with the prior of Hounslow, who offered to show me a prophecy; but
we had no leisure to speak together further, for we only met at the
new inn, where Mr. Yowng, Awnsam and his wife, and others,
dined with us. Skydmore also used to speak of young Sir Rice,
saying that Welshmen and priests were sore disdained nowadays.
As to Mr. Ferne, my wits were so troubled with sickness that I
cannot perfectly remember what he rehearsed; but by Mr. Bydyll's
rehearsal, Mr. Steward of Syon told me it was likely to be enacted
that no more tithe corn should be made. I was sick long after, and,
being aged and oblivious, did not see him till we met at the
Secretary's at the Rolls. Also Mr. Waren, old surveyor, and the
master of Ashford, in Kent, sometime steward to the bp. of
Canterbury, spoke in the churchyard of Istleworth of the hard
statutes made and to be made against the Church. Finally, I confess
the four bills by Mr. Feerne, Mr. Leeke, Mr. Skydmore, and Sir
Thos. Mody to be true, and that by such seditious ways I have
maliciously slandered the King and Queen and their Council; for
which I ask forgiveness of God, king Henry VIII., and queen Anne,
and shall continue sorrowful during my life, which stands only in
the King's will. "Moreover, Mr. Skydmore dyd show to me yongge
Master Care, saying that he was our suffren Lord the Kynge's son
by our suffren Lady the Qwyen's syster, whom the Qwyen's grace
myght not suffer to be yn the Cowrte."*

Seen in context, Hale was blaming Mr Skidmore (or Scudamore)
for suggesting that Henry Carey was the King's son. It was just
one of many libellous statements that Hale made, including that
Henry 'had meddled with the Queen's mother' and his actions
would lead to his execution in Tyburn later that year. But for his
accusation that Henry was the King's, he was the only person to
have been recorded at the time of spreading the rumour, whether
it was in fact truth or not.

At nine years old, Henry was unaware of the insinuation Hale had made about his parentage and his aunt was continuing to take his education very seriously. Nicholas Bourbon, a French poet, scholar and humanist that Anne Boleyn had saved from the French Inquisition was employed to give him tuition, which included learning the arts of rhetoric and logic, grammar, arithmetic, geometry and astronomy. Anne had been instrumental in securing Bourbon's release from prison and when he arrived at the English court, she paid for him to take up lodging with the King's physician, Dr Butts, while also employing him as a tutor for several of the wards of court.

Henry wasn't the only student of Bourbon's. He spent his days of scholarly pursuit with Henry Norris' son - whose father would be executed for his alleged indiscretion with Anne - and Thomas Hervey, both sons of prominent men of the Tudor court. He rarely saw his sister or his mother but his aunt Anne visited him in the December of 1535 and he came under her care until her downfall in 1536 and 'probably then returned to his mother and stepfather'[2] around the age of ten. Little is known of Henry's whereabouts during these formative years but his education must have continued, giving him the skills and ability to take up at position at court at the age of nineteen.

Life had settled down for his sister Katherine and she was concentrating on her family and motherhood. By the time Katherine was twenty one, she was the mother to four young children. Her daughter Mary had been born in 1542, the same year her husband Francis was made MP for Horsham, quickly followed by the births of Lettice in 1543 and William in 1545. These were days of the nursery so unlike the one Katherine had been sent to where she grew up with Elizabeth. This time Katherine was in charge.

Katherine and Francis had made their home at Greys Court, Rotherfield Greys, in the Chiltern Hills of Oxfordshire. Although King Henry had granted the couple the estate of Rotherfield

Greys around the time of their marriage, it took two further Acts of Parliament to secure their rights and for Katherine to be named joint tenant along with her husband. Greys Court was and still is a beautiful house with splendid gardens. Originally a 14th century castle with a fortified tower, a Tudor manor house was added and it was here the new Knollys family made their home. An incredible Tudor wheelhouse, operated by a donkey-powered treadmill to lift water from the well, was added in later years. Life was good for Katherine. It was a time for family and managing her own household; the kingdom was at peace but trouble was brewing.

Yet there was still time for a family celebration. Henry had joined the King's household by the time of his marriage in 1545 and he was a man who was ready to start his own family. Katherine might well have attended her brother's wedding to Anne Morgan, the daughter of Sir Thomas Morgan and Anne Whitney. Anne was of Welsh origin but was born and raised at her family's home in Herefordshire. It was a good match for Henry who was beginning to make his way in the world and it cemented his place at court. They probably had a typical Tudor wedding, conducted outside the church with the couple exchanging their vows and the bride being given a ring to wear on her wedding finger. Couples only really entered the church to receive a blessing. After they had left the church they would then travel to the bride's home where both families would celebrate the joining of their kin. It was also a chance for the families to show off their wealth and prosperity by providing food and entertainment for the assorted guests as well as distributing gifts to those gathered. The most exciting part of the wedding was the bedding ceremony that caused much mirth to the guests but must have left the bride especially somewhat embarrassed. Marriages were not deemed solid unless consummation had occurred, as we have seen with King Henry and Anne of Cleves, so making sure the couple were delivered to the bed chamber held great import as well as sport for friends and family. For Henry, it was a happy period of his life before he enlisted in the English army under Viscount Lisle, and accompanied him to France.

During this time, King Henry's health was taking a turn for the worst. The leg injury that had troubled him for so many years was constantly aggravated and infection was coursing through his body. Time was running out for Henry. By the end of 1546, he was in horrendous pain and spent most of his days bed-ridden. In his final days, Henry had made a will that caused controversy. He stuck to the Act of Succession of 1544 that gave the throne to Edward, followed by Mary and finally Elizabeth as long as the girls made marriages approved of by the Privy Council. Edward was left the bulk of his father's money and jewels and all his ships and artillery. The girls were made provision for by allocating them £10,000 in money and plate and £3,000 a year to live on. Of course, Katherine and her brother, Henry, were not included in his will, although he did grant small sums to his closest advisors. The controversy arose because the will was not signed in Henry's hand but was stamped. The use of a dry stamp was employed by his privy councillors as Henry's health was failing and he was no longer able to sign documents. It means Henry may not have been fully aware of what his will contained. Nor may he have been aware of the 86 documents that were also dry stamped in the month leading up to his death.

Henry was able to say his goodbyes to his wife, now Katherine Parr, and send her from his bedchamber and the place of his impending death. Lady Mary was also called for and in floods of tears, she agreed to look after her brother, Prince Edward, who was only nine years old and about to inherit the throne. Mary was about to be one step closer herself. The King was close to death but to talk of his demise was treason. No-one wanted to broach the subject especially with the King himself but it had to be done when it appeared that Henry was entering his final hours. It fell to Sir Anthony Denny, Chief Gentleman of the Privy Chamber, to warn the King that 'you are not like to live' and to urge him to make his peace with God. Archbishop Cranmer was sent for to undertake the last rites at Henry's bedside in his chambers at Westminster. On the morning of 28th January 1547, this once strong and proud King died in his fifty-fifth year, with his close confidant, Cranmer, by his side.

Henry's body stayed in his room for three days after his death. His demise was not proclaimed but kept secret while political wheels turned. His young son would have to be announced as King but his tender years meant that power play was afoot. Who would actually reign, managing the prince's decisions and advising and aiding him, until he reached eighteen? Edward Seymour, the brother of Henry's wife Jane and Edward's uncle, had been made executor of the deceased King's will. In it, there was no provision made for a Lord Protector to assist the young King but Seymour saw himself as fulfilling that role. The time taken between Henry's death and Edward's proclamation was spent in rallying his allies to him to convince the Privy Council that he should be Lord Protector until Edward came of age.

Seymour had already ridden out to escort the young prince Edward from his apartments at Hertford Castle to where Elizabeth was staying at Enfield to ensure that Edward was in his care and control. It was there that the two youngest children of Henry VIII were told of their father's demise and they clung to each other weeping for their loss. On 31st January, Edward was proclaimed the new King and Edward Seymour was firmly by his side.

Two weeks later, King Henry's body began its journey in a gilded chariot pulled by eight horses to St George's Chapel in Windsor. The roads from Westminster to Windsor had been cleared and cleaned to allow the four mile long procession to pass. En route, it stopped at Syon Abbey for the night where it is said that his coffin burst open and dogs licked at his remains. People were horrified not just because of such a terrible thing befalling their once great King but because it had been prophesised. A friar had predicted way back when Henry had chosen Anne Boleyn over Catherine of Aragon that dogs would lick his blood 'as they had done Ahab's' (Ahab being the seventh king of Israel whose blood was not only licked by dogs but by pigs according to the Greek translation of the Old Testament). To a superstitious people, this prophecy had the ring of truth and in the minds of the people, Henry's treatment of Catherine of Aragon had been judged.

Once the coffin was repaired, Henry continued on his journey to his final resting place alongside the wife he had loved the most, the wife that had given him his only legitimate son, Jane Seymour. King Henry was buried on 16th February in St George's Chapel at Windsor Castle with none of his family present apart from Katherine Parr who watched from the privacy of the Queen's Closet. After masses were said and Henry's coat of arms, helmet, shield and sword were placed reverentially on the altar, the service was ended with the proclamation 'Le roi est mort! Vive le roi!' The reign of Henry's son, the boy King, had begun.

The day before Edward's coronation on 20th February 1547, this young boy rode out from the Tower of London in great procession to Westminster Palace. The new King sat high on his horse dressed in white velvet decorated with lovers knots made from diamonds, rubies and pearls and covered with a sable cloak. Edward was led out by his gentlemen, trumpeters and chaplains on foot and behind them came the nobility on horseback. Edward Seymour rode in pride of place making sure he was always close by and the first to attend to Edward's needs. The following day they sailed to Whitehall by barge where Edward donned his kingly robes of ermine and crimson velvet, ready for his procession to Westminster Abbey and his coronation.

Archbishop Cranmer had been at work to make the

proceedings easier for the nine year old by shortening the service from twelve hours to seven. Rest breaks were allowed and cushions were added to the throne to raise him up before his people. For Cranmer, it was also a chance to herald in forthcoming religious reform. For once the new King was not to swear an oath to Rome. He was head of the church as his father had been before him but this time it was set from the moment of his coronation. Cranmer told the waiting congregation that there was no need to anoint the new King because he was already God's anointed: 'elected by God, the King was accountable only to God'[3]. Edward was crowned three times with St Edward's crown, the imperial crown and a crown made especially for the young boy. He was handed the orb and sceptre, St Edward's staff and spurs and allowed each of the nobility to come forward and kiss his left cheek. The coronation ceremony was complete.

And for Henry Carey, the perhaps illegitimate son of the dead King but at least the cousin of the new, times were changing. He moved into his new role in the political arena alongside Edward VI. When William Carey was alive, Henry had been granted the borough of Buckingham 'in tail male' - a grant that passed on to male heirs. In Weir's book about his mother, she suggests that this is one reason why Henry could not have been the King's. Entitlement could only pass down to legitimate heirs not bastard sons but as Henry was born in wedlock, regardless of whether he was the King's, this grant would still have passed to him. Henry Carey was elected MP for Buckingham and was present at the first Parliament of Edward VI's reign.

Katherine also had something to celebrate in 1547. She had given birth to another son, Edward, the previous year and her husband, Francis, was now achieving knighthood. Not only did this mean Francis was on his way to great and better things, she could now title herself as Lady. As with Henry, Katherine's brother, Francis had joined the new household of the young Prince Edward. He was sent North to Scotland with the English army and was knighted in the field at Roxborough by Edward Seymour, the now Duke of Somerset, Lord Protector and his commander-in-chief.

King Edward's reign was not a peaceful one. There was much social and political unrest, particularly in the area of religious reform. Cranmer was intent on making England a Protestant country and he had an ally in Edward Seymour. Cranmer pushed for change and Edward agreed in the most part to his ideas. The one who didn't and wouldn't refute her faith was Mary, her mother's daughter in every way, devout and unyielding. Living at New Hall, Mary was continuing to hear mass and flouting Edward's new rules. He was not amused. He may have been a boy King but he was still a King and Mary was being aggravatingly stubborn.

Whilst Edward and Mary were butting heads over religion, the Lady Elizabeth was living with Henry's last wife, Katherine Parr, the Dowager Queen, and was about to go through one of the most scandalous episodes of her life. Soon after her father's death, Elizabeth had joined Katherine at her residence in Chelsea. By mid-April, their household was also joined by Thomas Seymour, newly created Lord Admiral and the Lord Protector's brother and now Katherine's new husband. Katherine had loved Thomas way before her marriage to the King and now that he was gone and the Seymour family were in power, she could marry for love. But Thomas didn't have eyes just for his bride. He was more than a little enamoured with Elizabeth who was now a pert and attractive teenager.

Seymour stole the key to Elizabeth's bedchamber and used it to startle her in the early hours of the morning where he would pretend to dive at her leaving her shrieking and cowering in the corner of her bed. If she was up but not dressed, he became too familiar with her and would slap her buttocks whilst wearing nothing but his nightshirt. He stole kisses from her and flirted with her shamelessly whilst his wife, Katherine looked on. It is strange to think that Katherine would allow such behaviour. Perhaps she was afraid of losing Seymour's affections, but her behaviour became stranger still when she held Elizabeth down while Seymour cut her dress to shreds one day whilst they were walking in the gardens.

Katherine Parr was privy to Seymour's attention to Elizabeth but warning bells were starting to ring. When she caught them together in what seemed to be an intimate embrace, she asked her charge to leave her household. How far Seymour had got with Elizabeth, we shall never know but in May 1548, Elizabeth was sent to live with her father's gentleman, Sir Anthony Denny and his wife at Cheshunt. Still Katherine and Elizabeth stayed on good terms with letters exchanged between them frequently. In one Elizabeth wrote:

> *Although your Highness' letters be most joyful to me in absence, yet considering what pain it is to you to write, your Grace being so great with child and so sickly, your commendation were enough in my lord's letter. I much rejoice...with my humble thanks, that your Grace wished me with you, till I were weary of that country. Your Highness were like to be cumbered if I should not depart till I were weary of being with you; although it were the worst soil in the world, your presence would make it pleasant.*[4]

All the signs were that Elizabeth had encouraged Thomas Seymour at least to a certain degree. Being a teenager and in her first flush of attraction, she fell for the dashing Admiral and was swayed by his larger than life personality but she was no fool. She was still the dead King's daughter and as such acted with dignity in the days to come when her relationship with Thomas would come under close scrutiny.

Katherine Parr died eight days after she gave birth and was buried at Sudeley. It may have given Thomas some pause for thought but it wasn't long before he was dreaming up new ways to fulfil his ambitions. And this led him back to Elizabeth and the possibility of their marriage. He began to make enquiries as to Elizabeth's finances - ever the romantic(!), Thomas wanted to make sure she was worth marrying.

On 17th January 1549, Thomas Seymour was arrested and Elizabeth's servants Thomas Parry and Kate Ashley soon followed him to the Tower. They told their interrogator, Sir Robert Tyrwhitt everything about Elizabeth's conduct with Seymour. While shameful, it was not treasonous and Elizabeth was saved from further repercussions. Seymour, however, had gone too far. He had planned and plotted against the King, trying to usurp his rule to become more than he was ever likely to be. He was executed in early March and although it must have pained Elizabeth that the man she had been so attracted to was no more, she must also have sighed with relief to have not been tainted by his actions. It was an experience she would never forget, forging her resolve to remain a virgin although 'almost all the men that she subsequently loved, or pretended to love, resembled Seymour'[5].

Elizabeth managed to get through this time in her life - that included rumours that she had given birth in secret to Seymour's baby - and settled down for awhile in her new home with the Dennies. Her sister, Mary, however, was becoming a thorn in Edward's side. For her part she felt that the country was sliding into religious turmoil and ever the fervent Catholic, Mary felt it her duty to uphold her faith. She chose to hold four masses a day which was excessive to say the least but also infuriated the Privy Council. She was sent a letter requesting that she observe his Majesty's laws referring to the replacement of mass with a communion of the people and the use of the English Book of Common Prayer. Mary refused and wrote a furious reply in which she stated that the new laws were 'a late law of your own making for the altering of matters of religion, which in my conscience is not worthy to have the name of law'. The lord protector and the council could not allow Mary to disobey the changes to religious observation and summoned her chaplain and officers to a meeting in which they hoped they could convince them to make Mary see sense. Mary was not impressed and she wrote again to the Lord Protector:

My Lorde, I perceive by letters directed from you and other of the kings majesties Counsaile, to my Controller, my Chaplaine, and master Englefielde my servant, that ye will them upon their alleagaunce to repaire immediately to you, wherin you give me evident cause to change my accustomed opinion of you all, tht is to say, to thinke you careful of my quietnesse and wel doings, considering how earnestly I wryte to you for the stay of two of them, and that not without very just cause. And as for master Englefield, as soone as he could have prepared himself, having his horses so farre off, although yee had not sent at this present, would have perfourmed your request. Bit indeed I am much deceived. For I had supposed ye would have waited and taken my letters in better part, if yee have received them; if not, to have tarried mine answere and I not to have found so little friendship, nor to have bene used so ungently at your hands in sending for him upon whose travial doth rest the only charge of my whole house, as I wryt to you lately, whose absence therefore shall be to me & my saide house no little displeasure, especially being so farre off. And besides all this, I doe greatly marvaile to see your wrytinge for him, and the other two, with suche extreame words of pearill to ensue towards them in case they did not come, and specially for my Controller, whose charge is so great, that he canne not sodainly be meete to take a journey, which words in mine opinion needed not (unless it were in some verye just and necessarye cause) to any of mine, who taketh myself subject to none of you all, not doubting but if the kings majestie my brother were of sufficient years to perceive this matter, and knew what lacke and incommoditie the absence of my said officer should be to my house, his grace would have bene so good Lorde to mee, as to have suffered him to remaine where his charge is. Notwithstanding I have willed him at this time to repaire to you, commanding him to returne foorthwith for my very necessities sake, and I have geven the like leave to my poore sicke prieste also, whose life I think undoubtedly shall be putte in hazard by the wet and colde painefull travaile of this journey. But for my parte I assure you all, that since the king my father, your late maister and verye good Lorde died I never tooke you for other than my frende; but in this it appeareth contrary. And sauving I thought verily that my former letters shoulde have discharged this matter, I woulde not have troubled myself with writing the same, not doubting but you doe consider that none of you all would have bene contented to have bene thus used at your inferiours hands, I meane to have hadde your officer, or any of your servants sent for by a force (as yee make it) knowing no just cause why. Wherefore I do not a little marvaile, that yee had not this remembraunce towards mee, who always hath willed and wished you as well to doe as myself, and both have and will pray for you all as heartily as for mine own soule to almightye God, whome I humblye beseech to illumine you with his holy spirite, to whose mercy also I am at a full point to commit my selfe, what so ever shall become of my body. And thus with my commendations I bid you all fare well. from my house at Kenninghal, the 27 of June

Your frende to my power though you geve me contrary cause, Mary[6]

Her attitude was something she would carry forward into her later years and surprisingly it was allowed to pass. The council had far more important things to worry about, including the situation in Scotland, and Mary was left to continue her religious devotions the way she insisted they should be kept. Elizabeth and Katherine, now Lady Knollys, had been raised together in the Protestant faith and were of one accord when it came to matters of religion. Where Elizabeth and Katherine welcomed reform, Mary wanted a return to Rome and the Catholic religion. Her faith was her lifeline. It was all she had had to sustain her throughout her childhood and her separation from her mother. Her piety, devotion and stubbornness set the tone for what was about to happen.

Katherine and her brother, Henry, had begun to reap the benefits of their clouded births after King Henry's death and the reign of Edward brought them closer than ever to court. But when the boy King died at just fifteen at Greenwich Palace on 6th July 1553, it heralded a change in England that no-one had foreseen - the reign of Bloody Mary - and for Katherine it would mean uprooting her family and fleeing abroad.

Chapter Six

Bloody Mary and the Exiles

Mary fought for her right to the English throne and her fighting spirit was to transform her into a woman of power and vengeance; a woman that Katherine and her family would have to flee from. If there was ever even the hint of the acknowledgement of any blood between them, it would be swept aside with Mary's religious fury.

When King Edward knew he was dying, he wrote his 'Devise for the Succession' that disinherited his sisters, Mary and Elizabeth. He had hoped to pass the throne on to the male descendants of the Duchess of Suffolk, Frances Brandon, and failing that, to the male heirs of the Lady Jane Grey, but neither of them had any male children by the time of Edward's demise. Edward rejected the idea that a woman could reign by herself but on his deathbed his cousin Lady Jane was named his heir. Jane never wanted such majesty thrust upon her. She was merely a pawn in another Tudor plot for power, but one that Mary could challenge. To make sure Jane would be crowned Queen, her family and political allies set out to arrest Mary, who, always the shrewd one, had been clever enough to flee to East Anglia where she had support to her claim to the throne.

Mary wrote to the Privy Council from where she was holed up in Kenninghall, stating her case for her right to rule:

My lords, we greet you well and have received sure advertisement that our dearest brother the King and late sovereign lord is departed to God. Marry, which news, how they be woeful unto our hearts, He wholly knoweth to whose will and pleasure we must and do humbly submit us and our will.

But in this lamentable case, that is to wit now after his departure and death, concerning the Crown and governance of this Realm of England with the title of France and all things thereunto belonging, what has been provided by act of Parliament and the testament and last will of our death father – beside other circumstances advancing our right – the Realm know and all the world knoweth. The rolls and records appear by authority of the king our said father and the king our said brother and the subjects of this Realm, as we verily trust that there is no good true subject that is or can or will pretend to be ignorant hereof. And of our part, as God shall aid and strengthen us, we have ourselves caused and shall cause our right and title in this behalf to be published and proclaimed accordingly.

And, albeit this manner being so weighty, the manner seemeth strange that our said brother, dying upon Thursday at night last past, we hitherto had no knowledge from you thereof. Yet we considered your wisdoms and prudence to be such that having eftsoon among you debated, pondered, and well weighed this present case with our estate and your estate, the commonwealth, and all your honours, we shall and may conceive great hope and trust and much assurance in your loyalty and service, and that you will like noble men work the best.

Nevertheless, we are not ignorant of your consultations and provisions forcible, there with you assembled and prepared – by whom and to what end God and you know, and nature can but fear some evil. But be it that some consideration politic of some whatsoever reason hath hastily moved you thereto, yet doubt you not, my lords, we can take all these your doings in gracious part, being also right ready to remit and fully pardon the same freely, to eschew blood-shed and vengeance of those that can or will amend. Trusting also assuredly you will take and accept this grace and virtue in such good part as appeareth, and that we shall not be enforced to use the service of other our true subjects and friends which in this our just and rightful cause God, in whom our final affiance is, shall send us.

Wherefore, my lords, we require you and charge you, for that our allegiance which you owe to God and us, that, for your honour and the surety of your persons, you employ your selves and forthwith upon receipt hereof cause our right and title to the Crown and government of this realm to be proclaimed in our City of London and such other places as to your wisdoms shall seem good and as to this case appertaineth, not failing hereof, as our very trust is in you. And this letter signed with our hand shall be your sufficient warrant.

Given under our sign at our Manor of Kenninghall the 9th July 1553.[1]

Her letter arrived on the same day as Jane was crowned and showed the Privy Council that she was serious about her right to succeed. The lords of the council were in agreement with her claim to the throne and poor Jane, Queen of only nine days, was taken to the Tower along with her husband who had plotted to bring Mary down. In the coming days, Jane would be charged with high treason along with her husband Lord Dudley and two of his brothers at their trial in the Guildhall of London. All were sentenced to death. The evidence against Jane was presented in no doubt and presented to her in her own writing; she had signed her name as 'the Queen'. Though Jane had merely been a pawn in the Tudor game of politics, her life was now forfeit.

Elizabeth too was in a precarious position and she walked a dangerous line with her half-sister. Mary was now coming into her own power, one she felt was God given and she would have her own way. The relationship between these two sisters was set to change. It started well, with Mary making public shows of affection towards her younger sister, but Elizabeth knew it was only a matter of time before they would be at odds. Elizabeth had been brought up in the new religion, Mary stayed steadfast in her Catholic beliefs and it underlined the coming discord between them.

In a private audience between the two sisters at Richmond Palace, Elizabeth tried to patch the widening rift between them by asking Mary for instruction in the Catholic faith and to give her books so that she may read up on the ways of the old religion, it never having been taught to her. This satisfied Mary that Elizabeth was doing something to redress her religious mis-education, as she saw it, and she asked her to accompany her to Mass. It was noted though that Elizabeth 'tried to excuse herself, saying she was ill and complained loudly all the way to Church that her stomach ached, wearing a suffering air'[2]. Although Elizabeth would go some way to placate Mary, she would never be completely swayed by her or her beliefs.

Mary was crowned the rightful Queen of England on 1st October 1553 at Westminster Abbey and Elizabeth attended alongside the former Queen, Anne of Cleves. Instead of Archbishop Cranmer, the man who had heralded in Protestant reform, officiating over the service, Mary chose the Bishop of Winchester, Stephen Gardiner. It was a statement of her religious intent. Mary was coming into power in her late thirties and she had waited a long time to reign. Although Edward had tried to quash her religious practices, she was still a devout Catholic and she meant for England to reunite with Rome and to leave aside the Protestant reforms that her father had started and her brother continued.

Elizabeth was still trying to appease Mary but it galled her. She had probably heard by now that Mary was also discussing her behind her back, referring to her as a heretic and a bastard and reviving an old rumour that Elizabeth was in fact the daughter of Mark Smeaton. Mary said these things behind closed doors but as always gossip leaked out and Elizabeth knew her proximity to her sister was perilous. She asked to be able to withdraw from court but Mary refused to let her go.

Whilst Elizabeth was treading carefully with Mary, Katherine was managing to keep away from the changes at court and concentrated on raising her own family. In the years leading up to Mary's succession, Katherine had given birth to four more children; Maud, Elizabeth, Robert and Richard. All were born before 1552 and by 1553, Katherine was pregnant again. Her next son, Francis, was born on the 14th August when Katherine was twenty nine. Katherine had had ten children in twelve years. She was constantly in and out of pregnancy and childbirth and away from court but she stayed in contact with Elizabeth as much as she could.

Aside from her family duties, Katherine and her husband were practising Protestants which put them in direct opposition to Mary, the newly crowned Queen. Francis had attended the 1551 Eucharistic debates at the houses of Sir William Cecil and Richard Moryson and he was active in the furious discussion that centred around religious reform. With Mary on the throne now, the couple were also in a precarious position. As Katherine and Francis began to talk of leaving England, Elizabeth appealed to Mary again to let her go to her house at Ashridge. This time her wish was granted and for now, she could sigh with relief at being out from under the gaze of her watchful sister.

Mary could not immediately change worship back to the Catholic ways, however much she may have wanted to, but she wasted no time in starting the process. Many of the reforms that came before her accession were set in law and to change them meant a process of repeal. The First Act of Repeal was passed in Mary's first parliament and it abolished all religious legislation passed in her brother Edward's reign and reinstated the validity of her mother's marriage to Henry VIII.

But trouble was brewing. The people of England had welcomed Mary to the throne, believing she was her father's rightful heir and they too believed that Henry and Catherine of Aragon had been truly wed but when it became common knowledge that Mary wished to marry a foreign husband, Philip of Spain, discontent spread. Mary didn't just want a husband, she wanted a King to reign with her and many disagreed with having a Spanish King on the throne. Although Mary had managed to convince her Privy Council that she would marry no other save Philip, others were not convinced of the match and began to organise revolt.

Sir Thomas Wyatt along with Lady Jane Grey's father, the Duke of Suffolk, Sir James Croft and members of the Carew family plotted uprisings in different parts of the country. The plan was to take control of four separate regions and then combine their troops to march on the capital but the rebellions in the Welsh marches, the midlands and the south-west fizzled out leaving Sir Thomas Wyatt to carry out the rebellion in the south-east.

On 26th January 1554, Wyatt took Rochester in Kent and many local people rallied to his cause. The Duke of Norfolk was sent after him but his men joined Wyatt's troops swelling his ranks to around 4,000 men. Wyatt demanded that Mary should be put under his charge in the Tower of London and he began to march towards London. Mary, listening to her advisors, believed that Elizabeth had had a hand in the rising and she allowed her building resentment of Anne Boleyn's daughter to take firm hold. If Mary was to be placed in the Tower then it followed that Elizabeth would replace her as Queen and surely Elizabeth had some part in organising such a rebellion that would benefit her and put her on the throne. Mary wanted Elizabeth back from her retreat in the country so that she could be watched and dealt with as necessary. She wrote to her:

We tendering the surety of your person, which might chance to be in some peril, if any sudden tumult should arise, either where you now be, or about Donnington, whither (as we understand) you are bound shortly to remove, do therefore think it expedient you should put yourself in readiness with all convenient speed to make your repair hither to us, which, we pray you, fail not to do, assuring you, that as you may more surely remain here, so shall you be most heartily welcome to us. And of your mind herein we pray you return answer by this messenger.[3]

Mary had heard rumours that Elizabeth was about to move to Donnington Castle, a semi-fortified house, that could have been used to consolidate her position. She wanted her back at court but Elizabeth wouldn't budge. Elizabeth used illness as her excuse or perhaps she truly was ill, either way her reply was written by a member of her household and it stated that she was in hope every day of her amendment and would then repair to the Queen. Elizabeth was buying herself time, waiting to see which way the rebellion would end and for the moment, she was allowed to stay away from court as the situation worsened.

At London Bridge, Wyatt was met by a large force and cannon, many having rallied to support Mary after hearing her rousing speech in London's Guildhall. Mary had told the gathered people:

I am your Queen, to whom at my coronation, when I was wedded to the realm and laws of the same (the spousal ring whereof I have on my finger, which never hitherto was, not hereafter shall be, left off), you promised your allegiance and obedience to me.... And I say to you, on the word of a Prince, I cannot tell how naturally the mother loveth the child, for I was never the mother of any; but certainly, if a Prince and Governor may as naturally and earnestly love her subjects as the mother doth love the child, then assure yourselves that I, being your lady and mistress, do as earnestly and tenderly love and favour you. And I, thus loving you, cannot but think that ye as heartily and faithfully love me; and then I doubt not but we shall give these rebels a short and speedy overthrow.[4]

Wyatt's army waited for three days before it turned towards Kingston in Surrey where the bridge had been destroyed to stop his men from crossing the river. But they repaired it and marched on to Ludgate where Wyatt's men were overcome. Wyatt surrendered and was imprisoned in the Tower where he was tortured in the hope that he might incriminate Elizabeth.

Mary had had enough. She wanted Elizabeth with her immediately. She sent her commissioners, with a litter for Elizabeth should she still be unwell, to bring her to London. Once at Elizabeth's residence in Ashridge they entered her bed chamber and found Elizabeth in a state - probably more from fear than from illness. Doctors were called to pronounce whether she was fit for travel and when they confirmed that she could be moved she was bundled into a litter and taken to London - on the same day that Lady Jane Grey was executed.

Elizabeth was loved by the people and they came out of their houses to watch her procession into the city. Elizabeth, in fear of her life, and knowing that public opinion could certainly be swayed in her favour, played to the crowds. One hundred horsemen wearing scarlet coats rode before and after her litter. She drew back the curtains so that the people could see her dressed in virgin white, a pure and precious Princess of the realm. This did nothing to improve Mary's mood who at 37 was not the young and pretty Princess that Elizabeth was. When Elizabeth arrived at Whitehall, Mary refused to see her and she was sent to secluded and secure chambers, out of sight but close by.

Some of Mary's advisors, especially Renard, the Spanish ambassador who had filled Chapuys' position at court, were determined that Elizabeth should be sent to the Tower where she would be questioned further. On 16th March 1554 Mary finally acquiesced and Elizabeth was charged with prior knowledge of the Wyatt rebellion and informed she would be taken to the one place that filled her with dread and fear. The following day, a barge was arranged to take Elizabeth up river to the Tower. Elizabeth was petrified. She knew how Tudor politics worked only too well, how someone could be subject to trumped-up malicious charges and put to death with little evidence. If Mary wanted rid of her she would find a way and so she asked that she could write to her sister. In it she refuted the charges against her and pleaded her innocence. She wrote:

If any ever did try this old saying, 'that a king's word was more than another man's oath,' I most humbly beseech your Majesty to verify it to me, and to remember your last promise and my last demand, that I be not not condemned without answer and due proof, which it seems that I now am; for without cause proved, I am by your council from you commanded to go to the Tower, a place more wanted for a false traitor than a true subject, which though I know I desire it not, yet in the face of all this realm it appears proved. I pray to God I may die the shamefullest death that any ever died, if I may mean any such thing; and to this present hour I protest before God (Who shall judge my truth, whatsoever malice shall devise), that I never practised, counselled, nor consented to anything that might be prejudicial to your person anyway, or dangerous to the state by any means. And therefore I humbly beseech your Majesty to let me answer afore yourself, and not suffer me to trust to your Councillors, yea, and that afore I go to the Tower, if it be possible; if not, before I be further condemned. Howbeit, I trust assuredly your Highness will give me leave to do it afore I go, that thus shamefully I may not be cried out on, as I now shall be; yea, and that without cause. Let conscience move your Highness to pardon this my boldness, which innocency procures me to do, together with hope of your natural kindness, which I trust will not see me cast away without desert, which what it is I would desire no more of God but that you truly knew, but which thing I think and believe you shall never by report know, unless by yourself you hear. I have heard of many in my time cast away for want of coming to the presence of their Prince; and in late days I heard my Lord of Somerset say that if his brother had been suffered to speak with him he had never suffered; but persuasions were made to him so great that he was brought in belief that he could not live safely if the Admiral lived, and that made him give consent to his death. Though these persons are not to be compared to your Majesty, yet I pray to God the like evil persuasions persuade not one sister against the other, and all for that they have heard false report, and the truth not known. Therefore, once again, kneeling with humbleness of heart, because I am not suffered to bow the knees of my body, I humbly crave to speak with your Highness, which I would not be so bold as to desire if I knew not myself most clear, as I know myself most true. And as for the traitor Wyatt, he might peradventure write me a letter, but on my faith I never received any from him. And as for the copy of the letter sent to the French King, I pray God confound me eternally if ever I sent him word, message, token, or letter, by any means, and to this truth I will stand in till my death.

Your Highness's most faithful subject, that hath been from the beginning, and will be to my end,

ELIZABETH,

I humbly crave but only one word of answer from yourself.[5]

Mary was infuriated by the letter and it did nothing to change her mind. Elizabeth was taken to the Tower and she is reported to have said 'Here lands as true and faithful a subject as ever landed a prisoner at these stairs. Before thee, O God, I speak it, having now no friends but thee alone' as she arrived at Traitors Gate but it is more likely that she actually landed at the wharf and kept her own counsel. This way in would have been just as frightening as it took her past the lions in the menagerie and under the Bloody Tower where the scaffold on which Lady Jane had met her death was still visible in the courtyard. Elizabeth was housed in the apartments in the royal palace that had once been used by her mother and it must have terrified her to think that she too could be heading for the executioner's block at the tender age of twenty.

Members of the Privy Council came to question her but could make nothing stick. Elizabeth answered all their questions astutely and with great care, making sure that she said nothing that could incriminate her and lead to her death. Whilst she was there, the leader of the rebellion, Sir Thomas Wyatt, was executed but as he stood on the scaffold he exonerated Elizabeth saying, 'And whereas it is said and whistled abroad that I should accuse my lady Elizabeth's grace and my lord Courtenay; it is not so, good people. For I assure you neither they nor any other now in yonder hold or durance was privy of my rising or commotion before I began. As I have declared no less to the queen's council. And this is most true.'[6] His words could not save him and he was beheaded, quartered and his bowels and genitals were burnt before his head was placed in a gibbet at St James's which later disappeared.

Elizabeth stayed in the Tower until Sir Henry Bedingfield arrived. Seeing the courtyard busy with officers, Elizabeth felt that her time had come and asked if the platform on which Lady Jane Grey had been beheaded had been taken away, in fear that it still awaited her. The constable of the Tower, Lord Chandos, explained that the men were there to accompany her to her new residence - Woodstock, close to Oxford - a journey that took four days. As Elizabeth left the Tower people cheered, delighted that she was free but what they didn't know was she was swapping one prison for another. Elizabeth was under house arrest. Mary did not want to antagonise Elizabeth's supporters by keeping her in the Tower without charge but she still wanted her under her command and somewhere where she could be monitored.

Elizabeth continued to be uneasy. She stopped at Richmond Palace for a night on her way to Woodstock and was reported to have said that she was in fear of her life. She couldn't trust Mary or her council. Even though she was out from under the shadow of the Tower, she still felt her life to be endangered. Woodstock was to be her prison and home for the next year. It had been a fine palace once but had fallen into ruin and Elizabeth was made comfortable in the lodge there. She whiled away the time in riding and walking in the grounds, occasionally being called to court at Mary's whim. It was during this time that she scratched this short poem into a window frame:

Much suspected by me,
nothing proved can be,
Quoth Elizabeth prisoner.

During Elizabeth's house arrest, Mary was married to her Spanish Prince by proxy on 6th March 1554. Philip was a widower with one son and at twenty six was a good royal match but he also had no knowledge of England, very little interest in marrying a woman he referred to as his aunt, and with whom he would find it difficult to communicate, given that he spoke very little English. But aside from all this, he developed a soft spot for Elizabeth.

He asked Mary to show mercy and let her return to her own home. Whilst Mary may not have wished to soften her attitude towards her sister, she did want to appease her new husband. Elizabeth wanted to return to Hatfield but Mary was not going to let her go without talking to her first. The two sisters met one night in May and Elizabeth did her best to assure Mary that she had nothing to do with the Wyatt rebellion. Mary gave her a ring as a token of her affection and Elizabeth was allowed in the coming days to return home and end this troublesome period in her life.

For Mary, the rebellion did nothing to change her feelings about her Prince of Spain. Elizabeth was now irrelevant as she planned her future reign alongside the man she loved regardless of the country's feelings. She firmly believed that God approved of the match and on 5th July, Mary became Philip's wife at a full wedding ceremony held at Winchester Cathedral. It may have softened her temperament for a while. She had waited a long time to marry and was delighted at her new husband but it was not long before Mary pushed sentimentality aside and began her campaign of religious persecution.

The Revival of the Heresy Acts was passed in November of 1554 and read:

> For the eschewing and avoiding of errors and heresies, which of late have risen, grown, and much increased within this realm, for that the ordinaries have wanted authority to proceed against those that were infected therewith: be it therefore ordained and enacted by authority of this present Parliament, that the statute made in the fifth year of the reign of King Richard II, concerning the arresting and apprehension of erroneous and heretical preachers, and one other statute made in the second year of the reign of King Henry IV, concerning the repressing of heresies and punishment of heretics, and also one other statute made in the second year of the reign of King Henry V, concerning the suppression of heresy and Lollardy, and every article, branch, and sentence contained in the same three several Acts, and every of them, shall from the twentieth day of January next coming be revived, and be in full force, strength, and effect to all intents, constructions, and purposes for ever.[7]

Full force indeed. Mary was on a crusade to rid her country of those she saw as heretics, to restore the practice of saying Mass and to outlaw the Book of Common Prayer. One of the main people in her sights was Archbishop Cranmer, who had led much of the previous reformation and who, on a personal note, was instrumental in the divorce that separated Mary's mother and father and led to her mistreatment during her youth. Archbishop Cranmer had been sentenced to death on 13th November 1553 but in 1554, he was moved to 'Bocardo' prison in Oxford to await a further trial for heresy. Mary was certain to make an example of the one man she blamed above all other men for her previous unhappiness.

Many of those who had welcomed Protestant reform in

Edward's reign would flee to Europe. If they stayed in England, they would either be punished, put to death or made to convert to Catholicism. Hundreds of Protestants chose to relocate to Strasbourg, Frankfurt, Basle, Zurich and Geneva. In the July of 1555, Katherine gave birth to another daughter and her eleventh child, Anne, whilst Francis began to travel abroad, meeting with exiled Protestants and his friends and preparing for Katherine to join him. It seems that Francis had an early role to play as an envoy sent by Sir William Cecil, who would become one of Elizabeth's most trusted advisors, to establish where communities of Marian exiles would be welcomed. Their oldest son, Henry (Harry), joined him on a trip to Geneva as early as 1553 to meet Calvin, the great theologian and preacher, who wrote of him that he merited 'higher praise for piety and holy zeal'.

Back in England, the Second Statute of Repeal was passed in 1555 and built on the earlier repeal by nullifying any legislation that was anti-papacy apart from Mary's role as head of the Church of England. Things were getting increasingly difficult for Protestants still living at home and those that had the means made their plans to relocate to Europe, Katherine included. On 21st March 1556, Cranmer was put to death. He made his final recantation at a service at the University Church in Oxford where he was supposed to renounce his faith and admit that Catholicism was the one true religion. However, what he renounced were his previous recantations and he flatly stated that the Pope was Christ's enemy and furthermore the Antichrist. He was dragged from the pulpit and taken to the stake where he placed his right hand - the hand that had signed away his true faith - into the fire as the flames rose higher. Cranmer would die for his beliefs and he wanted those watching to know that he remained true to them until the end. It was a warning to those who still practised the Protestant faith and Katherine knew she was no longer safe. Francis made the move first, going to Basle in Switzerland around 1556, where he was recorded as a student at the university that was founded there in 1460, along with John Foxe, Richard Grason, John Bartholomew, John Audley and Richard Springham.

Katherine began her own preparations to flee from England. As she was getting ready to leave for Germany with five of her children, Katherine received a letter from Elizabeth. Elizabeth signed the letter 'cor rotto' or broken heart, showing how deeply affected she was to lose her friend, cousin and sister. The letter is dated to 1553 in Wood's *Letters of Royal and Illustrious Ladies of Great Britain* but Katherine did not travel to Frankfurt until 1557. Elizabeth must have sent her this note at a later date. One thing was certain, it was obvious that she would miss her and the two women whose lives were always to be entwined were saddened at their parting. Elizabeth wrote:

> *Relieve your sorrow for your far journey with joy of your short return, and think this pilgrimage rather a proof of your friends, rather than a leaving of your country, the length of time, and distance of the place, separates not the love of friends, nor deprives not the show of good will...when your need shall be most you shall find my friendship greatest...My power but small my love as great as those whose gifts may tell their friendships tale...*
>
> *Your loving cousin and ready friend cor rotto*[8]

Katherine's eldest daughter, Mary was now fourteen and she may have served Elizabeth while Katherine was overseas. The whereabouts of some of Katherine's children are not known at this time as only five made the arduous journey with her when she finally departed England in June 1557. Katherine's journey to Frankfurt was not the easy trip that can be made now but was a journey that could take up to six weeks, and she must have been worn out and anxious to settle into her new home, so far away from the country she had been raised in.

Frankfurt was a booming town populated by Germans,

French, Dutch and English tradesmen, many worked in the weaving trade and education and the production of books was also a thriving business with the yearly book fair being a main attraction. Charles V had offered the Marian exiles the freedom of the city but expected them to pay their taxes and take up employed work.

Katherine joined Francis, who was awaiting her in Frankfurt, to live in a house owned by John Weller, a wealthy merchant and burgher of the city. The exiles for the most part lived crammed together in shared accommodation. Katherine had her five youngest children with her plus a maid and they all had to fit into a household that included Weller and his wife, their five sons and four servants[9]. On 21st December they were admitted as church members into the Protestant congregation and settled down to life in a new country.

Mary's reign had continued and in just five years since she took the throne, she had burnt over 280 Protestants at the stake, many of whom were documented in Foxe's *Book of Martyrs* that would be published a year later. Foxe too had been in exile leaving England for Strasbourg in 1554 and moving on to Basle in 1556 where he had studied with Francis. He made it his life's work to write of the injustices of not just Mary's reign but of the continual persecution of Protestants. His book was a testament to why England should not be a Catholic country. And there was someone who agreed wholeheartedly - the future Queen of England.

Mary died in the November of 1558. Philip had long ago returned to Spain and she had spent her final months ill and unhappy. Her policy of religious persecution had done nothing to stop the tide of Protestant belief. Elizabeth was her successor and England was about to enter into a new and glorious reign.

Katherine and Francis could not have been more delighted. They could now go home along with the other Marian exiles and take up the life they had left behind. Francis actually returned to

England just before Mary's death to be ready to join the new Queen's court on her accession. Katherine came home too to join Elizabeth at court and closer still, to attend her in her privy chamber as one of her closest confidantes.

Chapter Seven

Queen Elizabeth's Lady

Elizabeth shed few tears for the sister who had imperilled her life and reminded her of the fate of her mother and how fragile Tudor life could be. Sitting underneath an oak tree at Hatfield, she received the news of Mary's death and was presented with her sister's enamelled betrothal ring as proof of her demise. Elizabeth was Queen.

Her first official words were in a speech entitled *"Words spoken by the Queen to the lords at her accession:"*

My lords, the law of nature moveth me to sorrow for my sister; the burden that is fallen upon me maketh me amazed; and yet, considering I am God's creature, ordained to obey His appointment, I will thereto yield, desiring from the bottom of my heart that I may have assistance of His grace to be the minister of His heavenly will in this office now committed to me. And as I am but one body naturally considered, though by His permission a body politic to govern, so I shall desire you all, my lords (chiefly you of the nobility, everyone in his degree and power), to be assistant to me, that I with my ruling and you with your service may make a good account to almighty God and leave some comfort to our posterity in earth. I mean to direct all my actions by good advice and counsel. And therefore, considering that divers of you be of the ancient nobility, having your beginnings and estates of my progenitors, kings of this realm, and thereby ought in honour to have the more natural care for maintaining of my estate and this commonwealth; some others have been of long experience in governance and enabled by my father of noble memory, my brother, and my late sister to bear office; the rest of you being upon special trust lately called to her service only and trust, for your service considered and rewarded; my meaning is to require of you all nothing more but faithful hearts in such service as from time to time shall be in your powers towards the preservation of me and this commonwealth. And for council and advice I shall accept you of my nobility, and such others of you the rest as in consultation I shall think meet and shortly appoint, to the which also, with their advice, I will join to their aid, and for ease of their burden, others meet for my service. And they which I shall not appoint, let them not think the same for any disability in them, but for that I do consider a multitude doth make rather discord and confusion than good counsel. And of my goodwill you shall not doubt, using yourselves as appertaineth to good and loving subjects."[1]

Historians differ as to whether Elizabeth gave this speech on 17th or on 20th November - the day she heard of Mary's death or the day she first met with her council - but by the 20th she certainly had other statements to make.

Elizabeth had immediately begun to consolidate her position by rallying her most important supporters to her side, including Sir William Cecil who was sworn in as her Secretary of State at her first Privy Council meeting on 20th November 1558. She told him:

I give you this charge that you shall be of my Privy Council and content to take pains for me and my realm. This judgment I have of you that you will not be corrupted by any manner of gift and that you will be faithful to the state; and that without respect of my private will you will give me that counsel which you think best and if you shall know anything necessary to be declared to me of secrecy, you shall show it to myself only. And assure yourself I will not fail to keep taciturnity therein and therefore herewith I charge you.[2]

Theirs was a relationship that would last for many years and, as Elizabeth consolidated one relationship, she also spared a thought for those other persons closest to her. Her childhood nurse and companion, Kat Ashley was made Chief Lady of the Bedchamber and Elizabeth began to form her court around her with those that she most trusted and loved.

Katherine and Francis were overjoyed at Elizabeth's accession. They returned to England along with many other Marian exiles to be a part of the new Elizabethan court and to see their new Queen ride to the Tower on 28th November 1558. Dressed in royal purple velvet and cheered on by ecstatic crowds, Elizabeth entered the Tower of London, never again to be a prisoner but now England's new monarch, ready to begin a long and powerful reign.

Where Mary Tudor had ruled with religious fervour, Elizabeth trod a more careful line. Protestants upheld her as their saving grace and a monarch who would stand by their beliefs. Elizabeth did lean towards the Protestant faith but she was ever the Queen of her people, a people who were both Catholic and Protestant and had seen enough persecution.

Elizabeth was still not able to acknowledge Katherine as her sister, as to do so would render Elizabeth herself illegitimate and therefore not the true successor to the English throne: to admit that Mary Boleyn had slept with King Henry would make his marriage to Elizabeth's mother, Anne, unlawful thus bastardising Elizabeth. Elizabeth knew the truth and she could welcome her closest kin to her side at court but she would never be able to acknowledge their true relationship. And she made certain that her Carey kin were well positioned around her.

In January 1559, Katherine was appointed as a Chief Lady of the Bedchamber - one of only four paid positions. Her second daughter, Lettice, was given a position in the privy chamber and her fourth daughter, Elizabeth, was placed in the Queen's household as a maid. Positions in the Queen's household were not easy to come by and Elizabeth only allowed the women that she trusted with her life to manage her care. Katherine's position in the bedchamber put her in the closest proximity to the Queen along with Kat Ashley and Blanche Parry - further evidence that Katherine was extremely important to the Queen and this shows that their relationship was an intimate one - as much as it was possible to be intimate with Elizabeth. The women of the bedchamber were responsible for dressing their Queen, washing her, cleaning her teeth and preparing her for bed, amongst other duties. It was hard work, being on call whenever Elizabeth should need them and she had to come first before anything or anyone else, including their husbands and children. After the women of the bedchamber came the women of the privy chamber - Elizabeth's day room - where she ate and received her most important guests. Lettice would assume her role here until her marriage to Walter Devereux, accompanying Elizabeth at court and in her quieter moments. The Queen's ladies were expected to dance, play music, read and embroider with Elizabeth, entertaining her and providing for her every need.

Katherine's eldest daughter, Mary, and third daughter, Maud, aren't recorded as being at court but it is safe to assume that they were serving in other ladies' households, possibly the Duchess of Suffolk's[3]. Katherine's sister-in-law, Anne Carey, joined the Knollys women with her daughters, Katherine and Philadelphia, in the Queen's household. The Carey and Knollys women were firmly ensconced by Elizabeth's side. And Katherine's husband and brother were also in favour. Francis was made a member of the Privy Council and vice-chamberlain of the Queen's household whilst Henry Carey was knighted and later made Baron Hunsdon.

The coronation of the new Queen had started with her symbolic taking of the Tower but it didn't proceed until the eve of 14th January 1559 when Elizabeth rode through London. The eve of coronation procession began at 3pm with Elizabeth leaving the Tower, carried on a litter covered in gold cloth, waving and smiling at the gathered crowds. The procession took her to

Gracechurch Street, Cornhill, Soper's Lane, Cheapside and Fleet Street where pageants were performed in her honour and her people gathered to see the plays and their new Queen. Katherine and Francis accompanied her - Katherine dressed in crimson and gold as were the other ladies-in-waiting who followed their mistress. Bundesen states that 'coronation livery was granted to Lettice Knollys, her sister Elizabeth Knollys and their cousin Katherine Carey' as well.

Katherine, Francis and members of their family watched on as Elizabeth was crowned the next day by the Bishop of Carlisle at a ceremony in Westminster Abbey. She began the day by walking in her crimson robes along the blue cloth that lined the path from Westminster Hall to the abbey. After listening to the sermon and taking the royal oath, she changed into clothes of silver and gold for her anointing. Donning a white tunic, she was then crowned with three crowns; St Edward's, the Imperial crown and a lighter crown (the Imperial crown weighing over seven pounds) that may have been her mother's[4] whilst sitting in St Edward's chair and also receiving the sword, ring, mantle, bracelets and sceptre of the realm. Changing again into a dress of gold, she sat on the throne to receive homage from the gathered dignitaries and listen to the Coronation mass but Elizabeth rose when the Bishop offered up the host - unwilling to conform to Catholic practices - and wearing her royal purple robe, she swept back to Westminster Hall for the coronation banquet. It was nothing but sumptuous and extravagant. Sir Edward Dymoke, the Queen's Champion, rode into the hall on his charger in full armour and challenged any one to a fight who would deny Elizabeth's right to reign. It was a romantic but serious political gesture and nobody made any objection. As for romance, that was something Elizabeth did not want to discuss.

Almost immediately Elizabeth was harried to marry by her councillors and even her ladies. Kat Ashley 'passionately implored her'[5] to marry for the sake of the kingdom and

Katherine must have talked to her about how married life could be. She had been married to Francis for eighteen years by now and had had another son, Thomas, in 1558 and was about to conceive another daughter, Katherine, who would be born in the October of Elizabeth's coronation year. But Elizabeth, as we know, saw herself as a virgin queen, married only to her kingdom.

Of any of the suitors that Elizabeth may have consented to marry, Sir Robert Dudley was the only one who captured her heart. Elizabeth's relationship with Robert, her master of horse, is now infamous but we shall never know how far their relationship truly went. Elizabeth favoured him above all other men and loved him in her own way. Early in her reign she may even have contemplated marrying Robert, even though he was disliked by many of her councillors, but the death of his wife brought down such a scandal that it quashed any thoughts of marriage the couple may have had. In the September of 1560, Amy Dudley fell down a flight of stairs and broke her neck - the circumstances were suspicious - she had sent all her servants out to the fair leaving her alone in the house. Was she secretly meeting with someone? Did she send the servants away so she could have alone time with Robert? There are many scenarios for what befell Amy but it is also believed that she had breast cancer and was in the final stages of the disease when a weakening of the bones can occur thus making her fall a fatal one. Whatever the circumstances of her death, it affected Elizabeth's relationship with her Robert. How could she marry him now when it was rumoured that she had a hand in his wife's death?

Also in 1560, Elizabeth granted Francis, Katherine and their son Robert the manor of Taunton in Somerset. Henry, Katherine's brother, was made master of the Queen's hawks and the following year was made a knight of the garter. Elizabeth remembered her childhood friends and family and was a generous Queen but there was also a harsh side to her, a selfish side - she was after all the reigning monarch. Katherine's relationship with Elizabeth made her 'often weep for unkindness'[6] and serving her sometimes kept her away from her husband and younger children. Katherine would have seen her daughter Lettice daily but during this year Lettice married and left court to live in Chartley, Staffordshire with her husband's family.

Somewhere Katherine and Francis found the time to be intimate together as Katherine gave birth to her last child, Dudley, named after Sir Robert Dudley, on 9th May 1562. Elizabeth was gracious in accepting the role of godmother as she was also to Henry Carey's daughter amongst others. Elizabeth demanded that any of her pregnant ladies should leave court to give birth but must return immediately, passing the child to a wet nurse for its care. Katherine saw little of baby Dudley. He died soon after his birth and Katherine and Francis were both devastated at the death of their baby boy. But Katherine had little time to mourn as Elizabeth was relentless in keeping her busy and life went on at court where she needed to be.

In the autumn of 1562, Elizabeth became frighteningly ill with smallpox. Lady Mary Sidney, Robert Dudley's sister, became her nursemaid and helped her back to health but she caught the disease and was so badly disfigured by it that she had to withdraw from court. Elizabeth seemed to have shown little sorrow or sympathy for her. By now she was a Queen who expected her people to sacrifice themselves for her - she was Gloriana. She may have been there for her people but she also expected her people to be there for her. They were hers to command and Katherine and Francis were no different, however close they were.

Francis had been appointed Governor of Portsmouth and one of his duties was to ensure that the men of the Newhaven (Le Havre) garrison received supplies and wages. He visited the garrison on several occasions but was then ordered to advise on their withdrawal. His position sent him not only to France but the Channel Islands and the Isle of Wight.

Katherine missed Francis but she had her duties to fulfil. Good news came when Lettice gave birth to her granddaughters Penelope early in 1563 and Dorothy in 1564. Katherine looked forward to seeing Lettice again when she briefly visited the court in 1565 but she infuriated Elizabeth by flirting with Sir Robert Dudley. Katherine's daughter had turned out to be a beauty and men commented on her looks and demeanour. Elizabeth was a jealous Queen and expected no woman to outshine her. Katherine's daughter was sent from court in disgrace but her relationship with Elizabeth would suffer more in the future. Dudley belonged to the Queen but Lettice had already turned his head and their relationship would blossom in years to come.

There was time for celebration in July when Katherine's eldest son, Henry, married Margaret, the daughter and heiress of Sir Ambrose Cave, the Chancellor of the Duchy of Lancaster on 16th July at Durham Place on the Strand. Elizabeth was guest of honour at the wedding. She had a soft spot for Henry and he was fast becoming one of the men she could trust and rely upon. She ordered a court tournament to mark the wedding celebrations but the joyous mood was not to last. Kat Ashley died on 18th July and Elizabeth lost her surrogate mother and closest friend who had been with her since she was a child. Katherine must have mourned the woman she had also spent part of her childhood with and had lately been her work mate but she gained by taking her place as Chief Lady of the Bedchamber. Francis too had continued his rise in position and power and was now given the role of Captain of the Guard. His position took him away from court and Katherine yet again. In 1566 he was sent to Ireland to advise Sir Henry Sidney, the lord deputy, on the O'Neill problem in Ulster and to control his expenditure amidst the turmoil of this rebellion. Francis was trusted by both Elizabeth and Sir William Cecil to undertake his orders, which he did although he didn't always agree with them. His most trying order was to come in

1568 when he was appointed guardian of Elizabeth's nemesis and cousin, Mary, Queen of Scots.

Mary was the daughter of the Scottish King James V and she had spent most of her childhood in France, marrying the dauphin in 1558 but when he became ill and died not long after his accession, she was left widowed. Mary returned to Scotland and remarried in 1565 but two years later her husband Lord Darnley was found murdered in his garden after an explosion had rocked his house. Some believe that Mary had a hand in his death although the Earl of Bothwell was also implicated. Matters were complicated still further when Mary married Bothwell and rumours abounded that they had conspired together to end Lord Darnley's life. There followed in Scotland an uprising against them and Mary was forced to abdicate and flee to England calling on Elizabeth to provide her protection. Elizabeth was no fool. Whatever Mary's involvement with Lord Darnley's death had been, she had also claimed that the English throne belonged to her. Elizabeth did protect her - by putting her under house arrest and who better to become her guardian but one of the people Elizabeth could trust above all others - Katherine's husband, Francis.

Francis was in his fifties now and beginning to wish for a life away from court and to be with his family but Elizabeth would have none of it. When Mary was moved to Lord Scrope's castle in Carlisle, Francis was sent to meet her. If Francis had to go, he wanted Katherine to go with him but Elizabeth refused as she 'loved Lady Knollys above all other women in the world' and could not bear to be parted from her.

Francis found Mary an intriguing woman from their first meeting. He reported back to Elizabeth:

We arrived here yesterday at 6 o'clock p.m. and by the way Lord Herries met us 6 miles from this town, discoursing much of his mistress's lamentable estate, her enemies' cruelty, her innocence of the murder of her husband, which would be easily proved, if she might be heard thereon before your highness—trusting also you would either give her aid to chasten her subjects, or leave to pass to France to seek relief. We said we doubted if your highness would like her to bring French into Scotland—and whether you could receive her so honourably to your presence as your affection to her wished, till you were satisfied of her innocence of the said murder. Whereon he seemed determined to ride towards your highness in a day or two—the thing we specially sought for. Then repairing to the castle, we found the Queen in her chamber of presence ready to receive us. Whereafter declaring your highness's sorrow for her "lamentable mysadventure, and inconvenyent arryvalle" though you were glad of her escape from peril: we found her to have "an eloquent tonge and a discreete hedd, and it seemethe by hyr doyngs she hathe stowte courage and lyberalle harte adjoyned therunto." After delivering your highness's letters "she fell into some passion with the water in her eyes," and taking us into her bedchamber complained that you did not answer her expectation to admit her forthwith to your presence, where on declaring her innocency, you would either without delay aid her to subdue her enemies, "or els beyng nowe come of good wyll. and not of necessitie, into your hyghnes handes (for a good and greatest part of hyr subjects, sayd she, doe remayne faste unto hyr styll)": you would at least give her passage through your country to France—not doubting but both the kings of France and Spain would help her. Here she said the cause of the war and treason of her subjects, was to keep that which she had so liberally given them, by violence, since by her privy revocation thereof with full age, they could not enjoy it by law. And "she affyrmed that both Lyddyngton and the lo[rd] Morton were assentyng to the murder of hyr husband, as it cowld wel be proved, althoe nowe they wo[ld] seme to perseque the same." To the first part we answered that your highness "was inward[ly] sorye and verye moche greved, that youe cowld n[ot] doe hyr that great honor to admytt hyr solempn[ly] and worthely into your presence, by reason off this great selander of

murder, wheroff she w[as] not yet purged. But we sayde we were
sure that your hyghnes affection towards hyr w[as] so great, that
whether hyr grace could purge hyr s[elf] or not in that behalffe, yet
yf she wold depend u[pon] your hyghnes favor, withowte sekyng to
bryng in stran[gers] into Skotland, (the ymmynent danger wheroff
your hyglmes cowld not suffer), then undowtedly yowre hghynes
wold use all the convenyent meanes youe cowld for hyr releeffe and
cumforte." And if it pleased her grace to direct us, we would
advertise your highness of her declarations with speed; and on your
answer, we should be able to declare your intent and meaning.
"Wherwith hyr grace complayned motche of delayes to hyr
prejudice, and wynnyng of tyme to hyr enemyes, so that discontent-
edlye she contented hyr selffe therwith." Wheron we took our
leave... [7]

Elizabeth was in no rush to agree to anything concerning Mary.
She was dangerous and Elizabeth knew it. Francis could
continue to monitor Mary and keep Elizabeth informed over the
coming months. His insistence that Carlisle Castle was not the
best place for her to be kept was agreed with and in July they
moved to Bolton Castle where Mary was housed in the south-
west tower. The castle was a cold, miserable place and tapestries
and rugs had to be borrowed from Barnard Castle and other
houses to make it more habitable. Francis did his best to make
sure he kept both Queens happy while all the while he wished to
be back with Katherine.

When he heard that Katherine had become ill with a fever
Francis asked for leave to visit her. He wrote to Lord Cecil in the
August of 1568:

As my wife has lately been sick, "and moderate travayle and
qwyatenes of mynd" are the only means to preserve her health, and
she is desirous to come hither if my return be not shortly, I desire
you to signify to her by this bearer whether it is likely I shall remain

here 5 or 6 weeks longer? For if it be, then with her highness's contentation (whereof I make no doubt) she will come forthwith; and if the likelihood be not, then I am sure it will content her. Her sickness has made my purse bare, and seeking health elsewhere cannot be without expenses, wherefore since I must needs be at charge, the same is best bestowed in satisfying her mind to the comfort of her spirits, and the healthful exercise of her body in travelling hither..[8]

But still Katherine was not allowed to join him nor was Francis allowed to visit her. And rumours had started about how Francis was being too lenient with Mary and how he had come under her spell. For his part, Francis explained to Cecil about Mary: *You see how she corrupts me, sending "tokyns" after me! That for my wife is a "pretie cheyne of pomander beades, fynelye laced with goolde wyer."[9]* Mary was doing her best to keep her jailor sweet, even by sending Katherine gifts. Given Francis' admiration of Mary, did Katherine feel pangs of jealousy at her husband being so far away and with this most powerful woman? Francis and Mary certainly had an interesting relationship. She referred to him as her 'schoolmaster' for helping her learn English and he allowed her perhaps more freedom than was wise. Katherine may have felt a little jealous but she was also feeling unwell again, her health was deteriorating and Elizabeth, so immune to other people's feelings at times, so strict with her ladies, loved her enough to care for her in her illness.

Francis often mentioned Katherine in his letters to Cecil even if it was just to excuse him for not writing to her. In December 1568, Francis thanked Cecil for good news concerning his wife - Katherine was well again and she implored Elizabeth to let her travel to Bolton to be with Francis but she refused fearing that 'the journey might be to her danger or discommodity'. But by 13th January 1569 Francis was thanking Cecil 'most heartily for comforting my wife in her "sycklye and dolfull estate."'[10]

Katherine's health had rallied but she was now failing fast and Elizabeth had her moved to a bedchamber near her own so that she could care for her.

Francis wanted to get back to Katherine even if it meant being subject to Elizabeth's wrath. He dreamed of a life away from court where they could retire to the countryside and live together as a family. He wrote on the 19th January:

> It seems by your letter you cannot promise my wife that I shall be discharged, but I trust you do not doubt it when I have brought this Queen to Tutbury—"for as sure as God is in Heaven," if I am not then discharged by order, I must repair to Court and suffer any punishment her majesty pleases. Save me that "obleqwye"—for if that is the fruit I shall reap for taking on me services that no man of my calling would have taken in hand, I will rather suffer such punishment as God lays on me, than adventure falling into such melancholy humours, as service in such a place might bring me to.[11]

But it was too late, Katherine died on 15th January at the young age of forty-four at Hampton Court Palace. When Francis heard the news he was devastated and for once unable to write to Cecil. He asked Henry, his brother, to respond to him regarding Mary, Queen of Scots and Henry began his letter with 'My brother being distracted with sorrow for his great loss... has desired me (to) answer to your last letter...'

Mary was moved to Tutbury in Staffordshire and is said to have blamed Elizabeth for Katherine's death. Elizabeth had definitely played a great part in keeping the couple apart and she was filled with remorse and regret, mourning her secret sister. Elizabeth felt 'passions of grief for the death of her kinswoman and good servant, falling for a while from a prince wanting nothing in this world to private mourning...'

Francis took time to mourn for the woman he had loved all her life, his wife and soulmate. He wrote to the Privy Council after her death:

I am much disquieted with this service in these strange countries, which melancholy humour grows daily on me since my wife's death. I am commanded expressly of God, "that I shall not tempte my lord my God," and my continuance here is intolerable, unless I obey man rather than God. My case is pitiful, for my wife disburdened me of many cares, kept all the "monuments" of my public charges, as well as my private accounts—now, my children, my servants and all other things, are loosely left without good order. But your lordships know all this without my rehearsal, and I leave it to your consideration.[12]

Elizabeth's grief and guilt and the knowledge she had lost one of the only women ever to be so close to her was shown in her orders for Katherine's funeral. She was buried in April in St Edmund's Chapel at Westminster Abbey. The funeral - 'almost a royal funeral'[13] - was paid for by the queen, costing £640.2s.11d (around £110,000 in today's money). A most fitting send-off for a woman who most certainly had royal blood. Katherine had lived through the reigns of Henry, Edward and Mary and had given her life in service to Elizabeth. It was right that she should be so honoured.

Thomas Newton published an epitaph to Katherine after her death:

Epitaphe upon the worthy and Honorable Lady, the Lady Knowles.

Death with his Darte hath us berefte,
A Gemme of worthy fame,
A Pearle of price, an Ouche of praise,
the Lady Knowles by name.
A Myrroure pure of womanhoode,
a Bootresse and and a stay,

To all that honest were, she was
I say both locke and kaye.

Among the Troupes of Ladies all,
and Dames of noble race,
She counted was, (and was indeede)
in Ladie Fortunes grace.
In favour with our noble Queene,
above the common sorte,
With whom she was in credit greate,
and bare a comely porte.

There seemde between our Queene & Death,
Contencion for to be,
Which of them both more entier love,
to her could testifie.
The one in state did her advaunce,
and place in dignitie,
That men thereby might knowe, to doe,
what princes able be.

Death made her free from worldly carke,
from sicknes, paine and strife,
And hath ben as a gate, to bringe
her to eternall life.
By Death therfore she hath receivde,
a greater boone I knowe:
For she hath made a chaunge, whose blisse,
no mortall wight can showe.

She here hath loste the companie,
of Lords and Ladies brave,
Of husband, Children, frendes and kinne,
and Courtly states full grave.

In Lieu wherof, she gained hath
the blessed companie
Of Sainctes, Archangels, Patriarches,
and Angelles in degree.

With all the Troupes Seraphicall,
which in the heavenly Bower,
Melodiously with one accord,
Ebuccinate Gods power.
Thus are we sure: for in this world
she led a life so right,
That ill report could not distaine,
nor blemish her with spight.

She traced had so cunningly,
the path of vertues lore,
Prefixing God omnipotent,
her godly eyes before:
And all her dedes preciselie were,
so rulde by reasons Squire,
That all and some might her beholde,
from vice still to retire.

The vertues all, the Muses nine,
and Graces three agreed,
To lodge within her noble breast,
while she in Earth did feede.
A head so straight and beautified,
with wit and counsaile sounde,
A minde so cleane devoide of guile,
is uneth to be founde.

But gone she is, and left the Stage
of this most wretched life,

Wherin she plaid a stately part,
till cruell Fates with knife:
Did cut the line of life in twaine,
who shall not after goe?
When time doth come, we must all hence,
Experience teacheth so.

Examples daily manifolde,
before our eyes we see,
Which put us in remembraunce,
of our fragilitie.
And bid us watch at every tide,
for Death our lurking foe,
Sith dye we must, most certainely,
but when, we do not knowe.

Som which today are lusty Brutes,
of age and courage ripe,
Tomorow may be layd full lowe,
by Death his grevous gripe.
Respect and parcialitie
of persons is there none,
For King, or Kaiser, rich or poore,
wise, foolish, all is one.

God graunt that we here left behinde,
this Ladies steppes may treade,
To live so well, to die no worse,
Amen, as I have saide.
Then maugre Death, we shall be sure,
when corps in earth is closde,
Amonge the joyes celestiall,
our Soule shal be reposde.

Katherine had lived too short a life and was sorely missed by the Queen, her husband and her family as well as those who knew and loved her.

Today there is an alabaster monument erected in her memory that can be seen in Westminster Abbey. Its inscription reads "The Right Honorable Lady Katherin Knollys Cheeffe Lady of the Quenes Maties [Majesty's] Beddechamber and wiffe to Sr. Frances Knollys Knight Tresorer [Treasurer] of her Highnes Howsholde. Departed this lyefe the 15. of January 1568 (Old style dating). At Hampton Courte. And was honorably buried in the flower [floor] of this chappell. This Lady Knollys and the Lord Hundesdon her brother were the childeren of William Caree Esquyer, and of the Lady Mary his wiffe one of the doughters and heires to Thomas Bulleyne Erle of Wylshier [Wiltshire] and Ormond. Which Lady Mary was sister to Anne Quene of England wiffe to Kinge Henry the Eyght father and mother to Elizabeth Quene of England".

Underneath it is a Latin inscription which when translated reads "O, Francis, she who was thy wife, behold, Catherine Knolle lies dead under the chilly marble. I know well that she will never depart from thy soul, though dead. Whilst alive she was always loved by thee: living, she bore thee, her husband, sixteen children and was equally female and male (that is, both gentle and valiant). Would that she had lived many years with thee and thy wife was now an old lady. But God desired it not. But he willed that thou, O Catherine, should await thy husband in Heaven".

Katherine had lived and died with the secret of her birth intact.

Appendix

Of Her Blood

Katherine's memorial plaque in Westminster credits her with having sixteen children; 8 boys and 8 girls, yet Francis's list of his children's births in his Latin dictionary gives us only 14 children; 8 boys and 6 girls. On Katherine and Francis's magnificent tomb in St Nicholas's Church at Rotherfield Greys, erected by their son William in 1605, there are seven sons on one side and seven daughters on the other with an infant by Katherine's side - presumably Dudley who had died at birth. There is a discrepancy with the number of daughters the couple had - was it 6, 7 or 8? It is quite possible given Katherine's fecundity that she had more daughters but that they died soon after birth or during infancy and thus were not recorded when Francis compiled his list.

Katherine's Children

Of Katherine's surviving children, **Lettice Knollys** was the most notorious. Lettice (also called Letitia) accompanied her mother as one of Queen Elizabeth's ladies but left court after her marriage to Walter Devereux, the 1st Earl of Essex, in 1560. Her marriage made her Countess Essex. Lettice had five children with Walter, one of whom died young. Her surviving children were Penelope, Dorothy, Robert and Walter junior.

Rumours surrounded Lettice when she attended court. She was an attractive woman with the red hair of her ancestors and smooth, pale skin. Gossipmongers suggested she was having an affair with Sir Robert Dudley, the Queen's favourite whom she had known for many years. Lettice was said to have flirted with him whilst heavily pregnant, sparking talk that the child could be his. Her husband was infuriated by the rumours which caused them much marital stress. When Walter died in Ireland, they were even more rumours and this time they were of poison. Had Walter's demise been hastened by Lettice's lover?

Lettice waited two years before she married Dudley, the exact amount of time that was appropriate for mourning before she became Countess Leicester. They were married in secret on 21st September 1578 at Dudley's house in Wanstead accompanied by only a few people including her father, Francis. Lettice wore a loose gown to cover up the fact that she was with child. Dudley was known to renege on marriage promises and so Francis may well have been there to make sure that the ceremony was conducted properly and the marriage was witnessed.

But of course Elizabeth found out. It is not certain who broke the news to her but she was furious that she had been so deceived. Lettice had her ears boxed and was banished from court with Elizabeth claiming that she would never be in the company of that 'she-wolf' again. Although Dudley returned to her favour, she would never forgive Lettice for her transgression of stealing her favourite away from her.

Lettice had several failed pregnancies with Dudley and a son who was nicknamed the 'noble imp' who was born in 1581 but his life was cut short, dying at just three years of age, much to his parent's distress.

When Dudley died unexpectedly, Lettice married the much younger Christopher Blount. It was a strange choice. Blount was a Catholic whereas Lettice had been reared in a Protestant family. He had for a time been her husband's master of horse but was knighted after his involvement in the fight for Dutch independence. They married in haste and this sparked rumours that Lettice had poisoned Dudley after he found out she was having an affair. It seems that vicious talk always surrounded Lettice. Elizabeth must have gloated at the way in which Lettice was constantly slandered.

Yet still she enraged her. Lettice was known to travel about with a huge entourage as if she were queen. She dressed her footmen in black velvet embroidered with silver bears, had her carriage pulled by four white horses and was followed by carriages of her ladies and servants. And Elizabeth still refused to have her back at court.

Lettice's son, Robert, from her first marriage, was however enjoying basking in the glory of Elizabeth's attention. He became one of Elizabeth's favourites after his step-father Dudley's death and he hoped to see his mother return to court. Lettice never gave up trying to win back Elizabeth's favour. She tried on several occasions to see her but was always left waiting while Elizabeth found an excuse to be elsewhere. Robert intervened and Elizabeth at last allowed Lettice an audience where she was allowed to kiss the queen's hand and breast and Elizabeth returned the embrace albeit with a frosty countenance.

But Robert's relationship with the Queen would take a deadly turn. In 1599, Robert was made Lord Lieutenant of Ireland and charged with the task of subduing a rebellion led by the Earl of Tyrone. Robert ended up making a truce with the rebels and returned to England to Elizabeth's fury. He was stripped of his offices and placed under house arrest. Robert tried to appease the queen but she further insulted him when she took away his rights to his income from sweet wine. Robert was in dire circumstances and he was an angry man. He began plotting his own rebellion to seize control of London, the court and the queen. In 1601, he was joined by his step-father, Sir Christopher Blount, as they marched on the city but the rising fizzled out and they were both arrested and executed for high treason. In a matter of weeks Lettice lost both her husband and her son.

Lettice continued on to live a long life, dying in her nineties. She had requested that she be buried with Sir Robert Dudley and she was duly interred in the Beauchamp Chapel of St Mary's Collegiate Church in Warwick.

Katherine and Francis were also parents to:

Sir Henry Knollys, the couple's first born son was a member of parliament representing Reading (1562 and 1571) and then Oxfordshire (1572). He was married to Margaret Cave (1549–1600), daughter of Sir Ambrose Cave and Margaret Willington. They had two daughters; Elizabeth who married Sir Henry Willoughby of Risley and Lettice who married William Paget, 4th Baron Paget.

He served as an Esquire of the Body to Elizabeth I and fought against the Northern rebels. On 16 January 1570, the Queen wrote to the Earl of Sussex and Sir Ralph Sadler asking that Knollys be awarded the rebels' lands and goods 'whom you know what reason we have to regard, in respect of his kindred to us'. But Henry was unlucky as the property had already been granted to Sadler's son.

In 1578, Henry joined Sir Humphrey Gilbert in a venture to set up a new colony in North America. Many of the ships that were to leave England were crewed by pardoned pirates. Henry seemed to get a taste for the pirate life and rejecting the venture, joined John Callis on a privateering expedition to the Spanish Coast. He was recalled to England after a foray to Portugal in 1582 and later left for the Netherlands where he joined in the fight for Dutch independence. It was here that he died after making his will that dealt mainly with the payment of his debts and the sale of his house in Greenwich.

Little is known of **Mary Knollys** although we do know that she married Edward Stalker.

Sir William Knollys, who became the 1st Earl of Banbury, was married first to Dorothy Bray, daughter of Edmund Bray, 1st Baron Bray, who was 20 years older than him and after her death he married Elizabeth Howard, daughter of Thomas Howard, 1st Earl of Suffolk and his second wife, Catherine Knyvett.

Like his father and brothers, William was an MP. He represented Stafford in 1571, Tregony in 1572 and Oxfordshire on four occasions up until 1601. He became warden of Wallingford Castle and was also once keeper of the Marshalsea. He was appointed Lord Lieutenant of Berkshire. He was a Captain in the fight for Dutch independence and was knighted for his actions by Sir Robert Dudley.

One story about William was that he followed his heart and it made him the butt of court jokes. He had fallen for Mary Fitton, the daughter of a family friend and made a fool of himself trying to attract her attention. His nickname was 'Party Beard' because his beard contained three colours; white, yellow and black and a song of the times went:

Party Beard, party beard...
...the white hind was crossed:
Brave Pembroke struck her down
And took her from the clown

Mary was pregnant with the Earl of Pembroke's illegitimate child but William still pursued her, much to the court's amusement.Later he became the 1st Baron Knollys and in 1616, the 1st Viscount Wallingford followed by his Earldom in 1626.

Edward Knollys was a Member of Parliament, representing Oxford in 1571 and 1572. He served in Ireland and died there.

Maud Knollys like her sister, Mary, remains a mystery.

Elizabeth Knollys attended on Queen Elizabeth I as a maid and then as a lady of the privy chamber, receiving a yearly salary of £33 6s 8d. She married Sir Thomas Leighton of Feckenham, Worcester, son of John Leighton of Watlesburgh and Joyce Sutton in 1578. Her husband served as Governor of Jersey and Guernsey but Elizabeth spent most of her time at court.

It is said that Sir Walter Raleigh was enamoured by her and wrote her a poem which she found in her pocket. It read 'Lady, farewell, whom I in silence serve!/Would God thou knews't the depth of my desire!/Then might I hope, though naught I can deserve,/Some drop of grace should quench my scalding fire.../

She had three children: Thomas, Elizabeth and Anne.

Sir Robert Knollys was a Member of Parliament representing Reading, Berkshire (1572–1589) and Breconshire (1589–1604). He married Catherine Vaughan, daughter of Sir Rowland Vaughan, of Porthamel with whom he had two daughters, Lettice and Frances.

Robert was keeper of Syon House from 1584-7 as well as being keeper of Crown lands in the surrounding area. He was a Gentleman of the Privy Chamber and an Esquire of the Body. In the 1580s, Blanche Parry, one of Elizabeth's chief women, challenged his right to his Breconshire estate (accessed through his wife) and stated that he had gained it through 'wicked, ungodly and abominable practices'. He still remained in Elizabeth's favour however and continued to be active at court and in parliament on the accession of James I.

Robert tried different ways of making money throughout his life, like applying for a licence to dye and transport silks but he was constantly in debt. After a fall at William's house from which he never recovered, he died owing more than £500.

Richard Knollys was a Member of Parliament representing first Wallingford (1584) and possibly Northampton (1588). He married Joan Heigham, daughter of John Heigham, of Gifford's Hall, Wickhambrook, Suffolk.

Sir Francis Knollys 'the Younger' was also a Member of Parliament, representing first Oxford (1572–1588) and then Berkshire (1597, 1625) and Reading. He married Lettice Barrett, daughter of John Barrett, of Hanham in 1588. They had three sons and six daughters.

Francis was a privateer serving as a rear admiral in the Caribbean with Sir Francis Drake. He also joined the fight for Dutch independence and was knighted in the field at Flushing in 1587.

At his death in 1648 he was described as being 'the ancientist Parliament man in England' after serving for 73 years. He was buried in the church of St Lawrence in Reading.

Anne Knollys married Thomas West, 2nd Baron De La Warr. They had six sons and eights daughters including Thomas West, 3rd Baron De La Warr, after whom the state of Delaware is named.

Sir Thomas Knollys married Odelia de Morana, daughter of John de Morada, Marquess of Bergen with whom he had a daughter, Penelope. He became Governor of Ostend in 1586 and served in the fight for Dutch independence also known as the Eighty Years' War (1568–1648).

Katherine Knollys married into an Irish family. Her husband Gerald FitzGerald, Baron of Offaly, was the son of Gerald FitzGerald, 11th Earl of Kildare and Mabel Browne. After his death she married Sir Phillip Boteler or Butler, of Watton Woodhall. She was the mother of Lettice Digby, 1st Baroness Offaly by her first husband and four sons by her second including Sir John Boteler and Sir Robert Boteler.

Francis went on after Katherine's death to have a long and illustrious career at court and in 1593 he received the Order of the Garter. He mourned Katherine for many years but his children and grandchildren kept him busy, bringing him great delight, troubles to remedy and never a dull moment. He died in the summer of 1596 leaving a will in which he said 'forasmuch as my goods are not sufficient to supply the wants and necessities of my children', there should be no 'costly pomp of ceremonies or great gifts of blacks for mourning at my burial, whereby my children might anyways be hindered'.

Because of Mary Boleyn, Henry VIII's bloodline has continued on through the centuries. Katherine and her brother Henry's descendants include Charles Darwin, Sir Winston Churchill, P G Wodehouse, Lord Nelson, Sarah Ferguson, Duchess of York, Camilla Parker Bowles, Duchess of Cornwall, Diana Spencer, Princess of Wales, Queen Elizabeth II and Kate Middleton, Duchess of Cambridge.

References

Chapter One - Mother Mary
1. Calendar of State Papers Relating to English Affairs in the Archives of Venice, Volume 2: 1509-1519, 508
2. Letters and Papers, Foreign and Domestic, of the Reign of Henry VIII
3. Sim, Alison: *The Tudor Housewife*
4. Letters and Papers, Foreign and Domestic, of the Reign of Henry VIII
5. *The Love Letters of Henry VIII* (ed. Jasper Ridley, 1988)
6. Ibid

Chapter Two - Aunty Anne
1. *The Love Letters of Henry VIII* (ed. Jasper Ridley, 1988)
2. Quoted in The Anne Boleyn Papers (Elizabeth Norton)
3. Ibid
4. Erickson, *The First Elizabeth*
5. Letters and Papers, Foreign and Domestic, Henry VIII, Volume 6, 1533
6. Calendar of State Papers, Spain, Volume 4, pt2
7. Letters and Papers, Foreign and Domestic, Henry VIII, Volume 7, 1534
8. Letters and Papers, Foreign and Domestic, Henry VIII, Volume 10, 1536

Chapter Three - Growing Up with Elizabeth and Mary
1. Letters and Papers, Foreign and Domestic, Henry VIII, Volume 11, 1536
2. Letters and Papers, Foreign and Domestic, Henry VIII, Volume 11, 1536
3. Letters and Papers, Foreign and Domestic, Henry VIII, Volume 11, 1536

Chapter Four - Maid of Honour

1. Letters and Papers, Foreign and Domestic, Henry VIII, Volume 14 Part 2: August-December 1539
2. Hall, *The Triumphant Reign of King Henry Eighth*
3. Ibid
4. Ibid
5. Merriman, *Life and Letters of Thomas Cromwell*
6. Strype, *Ecclesiastical Memorials of Henry VIII, Edward VI and Mary I*
7. Ibid
8. www.theanneboleynfiles.com
9. Strype, *Ecclesiastical Memorials of Henry VIII, Edward VI and Mary I*
10. Letters and Papers, Foreign and Domestic, Henry VIII, Volume 15, 1540
11. Wood, *Letters of Royal and Illustrious Ladies*
12. Quoted in Weir, *The Six Wives of Henry VIII*
13. Ibid

Chapter Five - The Two Henrys

1. Calendar of State Papers Relating to English Affairs in the Archives of Venice, Volume 4: 1527-1533
2. Hart, *Mistresses of Henry VIII*
3. Starkey, *The Young Elizabeth*
4. Hearne, *Sylloge*
5. Starkey, *The Young Elizabeth*
6. Foxe, *Acts and Monuments*

Chapter Six - Bloody Mary and the Exiles

1. Foxe, *Acts and Monuments*
2. Calendar of State Papers, Spain, Volume 11
3. Hearne, *Sylloge*
4. *Foxe, Actes and Monuments*
5. Harrison, G. B., ed. *The Letters of Queen Elizabeth I*

6. Starkey, *The Young Elizabeth*
7. Gee, H and Hardy W J (eds), *Documents Illustrative of English Church History*
8. Green, *Letters of Illustrious Ladies*
9. Garrett, *The Marian Exiles*

Chapter Seven - Queen Elizabeth's Lady

1. *Elizabeth I: Collected Works*
2. Read, *Mr Secretary Cecil and Queen Elizabeth*
3. Bundesen, unpublished thesis
4. Somerset, *Elizabeth I*
5. Ibid
6. Knollys, Papers, 65
7. Calendar of State Papers, Scotland
8. Ibid
9. Ibid
10. Ibid
11. Ibid
12. Ibid
13. Weir, *Mary Boleyn*

Bibliography

Primary Sources

Cecil Papers

Foxe, John: *History of the Acts and Monuments of the Church (Fox's Book of Martyrs)*, London, 1563

Hall, Edward: *The Triumphant Reign of King Henry Eighth*, London, 1547

Letters of the Queens of England 1100-1547, ed. Anne Crawford, Stroud, 1994

Newton, Thomas: *Epitaphe upon the worthy and Honorable Lady, the Lady Knowles*, London, 1569

Letters and Papers, Foreign and Domestic, of the Reign of Henry VIII

Merriman, RB (ed), *Life and Letters of Thomas Cromwell*, Oxford, 1902

Papers relating to Mary Queen of Scots, ed. William Knollys, Philobiblon Society

Miscellanies, 14-15, 1872-6

Calendar of State Papers, Domestic (Edward, Mary and Elizabeth)

Calendar of State Papers, Foreign

Calendar of State Papers, France

Calendar of State Papers, Ireland

Calendar of State Papers, Scotland

Calendar of State Papers, Venice

Strype, *Ecclesiastical Memorials of Henry VIII, Edward VI and Mary I*, London, 1816

The Privy Purse Expenses of King Henry the Eighth from November MDXIX to December MDXXXII, ed. Sir Nicholas Harris, London, 1827

The Love Letters of Henry VIII, ed. Jasper Ridley, 1988

Letters of Royal and Illustrious Ladies of Great Britain, Mary Anne Everett Wood, London, 1846

Secondary Sources

Ackroyd, Peter: *Tudors*, London, 2012

Ashdown, Dulcie M: *Ladies-in-Waiting*, London, 1976

Bernard, GW: *Anne Boleyn: Fatal Attractions*, Yale, 2010

Bernard, GW: *The King's Reformation: Henry VIII and the Making of the English Church*, London, 2007

Borman, Tracy: *Elizabeth's Women*, London, 2009

British History Online, www.british-history.ac.uk

Bundesen, Kristin: 'No other faction but my own: dynastic politics and Elizabeth I's Carey Cousins', unpublished thesis, 2008

Denny, Joanna: *Anne Boleyn*, London, 2004

Denny, Joanna: *Katherine Howard*, London, 2005

Dewhurst, John: 'The Alleged Miscarriages of Catherine of Aragon and Anne Boleyn', *Medical History*, 1984, 28, p49-56

Dunn, Jane: *Elizabeth & Mary*, London, 2003

Erickson, Carolly: *The First Elizabeth*, London, 1999

Fox, Julia: *Jane Boleyn*, London, 2007

Fraser, Antonia: *The Six Wives of Henry VIII*, London, 1992

Fraser, Antonia: *Mary Queen of Scots*, London, 1969

Froude, James: *The Reign of Mary Tudor*, London,1910

Garrett, Christina Hallowell: *The Marian Exiles*, Cambridge, 1938

Guy, John: *The Children of Henry VIII*, Oxford, 2013

Guy, John: *Tudor England*, Oxford, 1998

Hart, Kelly: *Mistresses of Henry VIII*, London, 2009

Hoskins, Anthony: 'Mary Boleyn's Carey Children - Offspring of Henry VIII?' *Genealogy Magazine*, Vol. 25, March 1997, No.9

Ives, Eric: *The Life and Death of Anne Boleyn*, Oxford, 2004

Hasler, PW (ed): 'The Role of the Marian Exiles' in *The History of Parliament: the House of Commons 1558-1603*. Available from the History of Parliament Online

Hume, Martin Andrew Sharp: *The Wives of Henry the Eighth and the Parts They Played in History*, London, 1905

Jones, Philippa: *The Other Tudors*, London, 2009

Laurence, Anne: *Women in England 1500-1760 A Social History,* London, 1994

Loades, David: *Henry VIII: King and Court,* Andover, 2009

Loades, David: *Mary Tudor,* Oxford, 1989

Loades, David: *The Politics of Marriage: Henry VIII and his Queens,* Stroud, 1994

Meyer, GJ: *The Tudors,* New York, 2010

Mortimer, Ian: *The Time Traveller's Guide to Elizabethan England,* London, 2012

Murphy, Beverley: *Bastard Prince: Henry VIII's Lost Son,* Stroud, 2001

Norton, Elizabeth: *Anne of Cleves,* Stroud, 2010

Norton, Elizabeth: *England's Queens,* Stroud, 2012

Norton, Elizabeth: *The Anne Boleyn Papers,* Stroud, 2013

Norton, Elizabeth: *The Boleyn Women,* Stroud, 2013

Parliament Online, www.historyofparliamentonline.org

Parmiter, Geoffrey de C: *The Kings Great Matter,* London, 1967

Perry, Maria: *The Word of a Prince: A Life of Elizabeth I,* Woodbridge, 1990

Plowden, Alison: *The Young Elizabeth,* Stroud, 1971

Plowden, Alison: *Tudor Women,* London, 1979

Porter, Linda: *Mary Tudor: The First Queen,* London, 2007

Read, Conyers: *Mr Secretary Cecil and Queen Elizabeth,* London, 1955

Rex, Richard: *Henry VIII,* Stroud, 2009

Rex, Richard: *The Tudors,* Stroud, 2002

Ridgway, Claire: *The Anne Boleyn Collection,* 2012

Ridley, Jasper: *Elizabeth I,* London, 1987

Ridley, Jasper: *Henry VIII,* London, 1984

Ridley, Jasper: *The Life and Times of Mary Tudor,* London, 1973

Ridley, Jasper: *The Tudor Age,* London, 1988

Scarisbrick, JJ: *Henry VIII,* London, 1997

Sim, Alison: *Pleasures and Pastimes in Tudor England,* Stroud, 2009

Sim, Alison: *The Tudor Housewife,* Stroud, 2010

Starkey, David: *Elizabeth*, London, 2000

Starkey, David: *Monarchy*, London, 2006

Starkey, David: *Six Wives: The Queens of Henry VIII*, London, 2003

Somerset, Anne: *Elizabeth I*, London, 1991

Somerset, Anne: *Ladies in Waiting*, London, 1984

Thurley, Simon: *The Palaces of Tudor England*, Yale, 1993

Varlow, Sally: *Lady Penelope*, London, 2007

Varlow, Sally: 'Sir Francis Knollys' Latin Dictionary: New Evidence for Katherine Carey', *Bulletin of the Institute of Historical Research*, 2006

Weir, Alison: *Elizabeth the Queen*, London, 1998

Weir, Alison: *The Lady in the Tower*, London, 2009

Weir, Alison: *The Six Wives of Henry VIII*, London, 1991

Weir, Alison: *Mary Boleyn*, London, 2011

Whitelock, Anna: *Elizabeth's Bedfellows*, Bloomsbury, 2013

Wilkinson, Josephine: *Mary Boleyn*, Stroud, 2009

Chronos Books is a historical non-fiction imprint. Chronos
publishes real history for real people; bringing to life historical
people, places and events in an imaginative, easy-to-digest and
accessible way. We want writers of historical books, from ancient
times to the Second World War, that will add to our
understanding of people and events rather than being
a dry textbook; history that passes on its stories to
a generation of new readers.